RHYMING HISTORY

The Story of England in Verse

RHYMING HISTORY
The Story of England in Verse

by Colin Wakefield

Illustrations by John Partridge

VOLUME TWO: 1485 – 1603

The Tudors

DHP
Double Honours Publications

RHYMING HISTORY
The Story of England in Verse

VOLUME TWO: 1485 – 1603
The Tudors

First published in 2012 by Double Honours Publications.

ISBN 978-0-9570120-1-1

Double Honours Publications

Email: info@rhyminghistory.co.uk
Website: www.rhyminghistory.co.uk

Printed and bound by Short Run Press, Exeter

AUTHOR'S NOTE

This is Volume Two of a longer *Rhyming History* of mine (still in the writing), which will eventually stretch from Julius Caesar's invasion of Britain in 55BC to the present day.

Volume Three (James I and Charles I) will appear in 2013, with subsequent volumes published annually. All published volumes are available for sale through the website.

I had no great success with history at school, so set about educating myself in later life. These books of verse are directed at people like me who want to learn about our history, but in not too solemn a way. I hope they will also appeal to a wider audience, students and historians, and those who simply enjoy reading poetry.

John Partridge has provided witty and entertaining illustrations to accompany the text, for which I am most grateful.

Special thanks to Jonathan Dowie for preparation of the text, Chris Moss for help with the cover, Christopher Dowie and Anne Reid for advice on the text, and Michael Callahan and Chris Wakefield for invaluable support.

Please visit our website for updates on future volumes of the *History*, and for news of live performances of the verse.

www.rhyminghistory.co.uk

Colin Wakefield – July 2012

HENRY THE SEVENTH (1485 – 1509)

Henry Tudor, in 1485,   **1485**
Took an historic risk. Few men alive
Would offer odds against Richard the Third.
At Bosworth Field, however, undeterred,
Henry, Earl of Richmond, with a small force,
Robbed Richard of his kingdom *and* his horse.

The King's supporters, too ashamed to fight,
Deserted him in droves. His greater might
Availed him not a jot: the rising star
Was Richmond. Men saluted him. "Hurrah!" –
They cried, "Long live King Henry!" The gold crown
Was spotted in a thorn bush, dusted down
And polished up, then placed on Henry's head –
There, on the battlefield, where Richard lay dead.

Henry's claim

All this euphoria suited him fine,
But his claim was fragile. His royal line

(Lancastrian) went back to John of Gaunt,
On his mother's side. But he couldn't flaunt
This connection. His mother, Margaret,
Was John of Gaunt's great-granddaughter, and yet
His great-great-grandmother wasn't Gaunt's wife
When she gave birth. Now, you can bet your life
The Yorkists would have exploited this fact,
And with relish, had the King voiced it. Tact,
In some measure, was what Henry needed.
His lineage went largely unheeded.
He simply claimed the crown as his by right,
And by judgement of God. To his delight,
Parliament (which he summoned) agreed,
Confirming the new King's right to succeed.
This took place after his coronation,
Thereby demonstrating to the nation
That Parliament was ratifying,
Not granting, his authority. Satisfying...

...And smart. King Henry the Seventh had brains.
Right from the start he took the greatest pains
To shore up his insecure position,
Wrong-footing the Yorkist opposition
With *finesse.* He sealed his opponents' fate
With a declaration that the true date
Of his accession was the day before
His victory at Bosworth, and therefore
His enemies were traitors to the King.
Clever, eh? Henry thought of everything.

He also planned his marriage with care.
Even pre-Bosworth he was well aware
Of the need to woo Yorkists. He was right.
White Rose dissidents joined him in the fight
Against Richard. In return he agreed
That, should his campaign for the crown succeed,
He'd wed Edward the Fourth's eldest daughter,
Elizabeth. Many a supporter

The Tudors

He won in this way. It has to be said
That this alliance of White Rose and Red
Did more to end the bloody civil wars
Than anything else, and merits applause.

The new King was still careful, however,
Not to hurry his marriage. He'd never,
Ever, allow malign speculation
From a snide and disrespectful nation;
Never allow gossip and idle talk
That his alliance with the House of York
Legitimised his kingship. He delayed
The wedding for five months and thus displayed,   **1486**
Yet again, his sound judgement and sure touch.
Happily, he loved his new wife very much.

Despite the weakness of his royal claim,
There was no other significant name
That was stronger – Lancastrian, at least.
Of Yorkist blood, with Richard now 'deceased'
(Also his young son), there were very few.

Richard himself had done away with two:
Edward the Fourth's unfortunate young sons,
In the Tower. They weren't the only ones,
However, who could claim direct descent
From Edward the Third. Still left to torment
Henry was the Duke of Clarence's son,
The Earl of Warwick: claimant Number One.

At ten years old, however, a mere boy,
He posed no present threat. Many a ploy,
Though, was cooked up in poor young Warwick's name –
None of them successful, but all the same
Dangerous and distracting for the King.
Two, in particular, were quite menacing.

3

Rhyming History

Lambert Simnel

Lambert Simnel was only twelve years old,
A gentle, humble lad, or so we're told.
An Oxford priest, his tutor, had this dream
Of passing Lambert off (a hare-brained scheme)
As Edward, Earl of Warwick, having heard
That the true Earl had lately died. Absurd,
I know, but bear in mind how very weak
The King remained. This plot (a shocking cheek)
Nevertheless attracted supporters
From a range of most unlikely quarters –
From Ireland in particular, the north,
And Cornwall. But the true Earl was brought forth
And paraded, in a show of fitness,
Through the London streets: Henry's star witness.

Still, in Dublin, Simnel was proclaimed King:
Edward the Sixth – crowned and everything.
This was 1487, in May,   **1487**
And in June he landed, in full array,
In England, to assert his so-called 'right'.

A rag-bag of old Yorkists joined the fight:
The Earl of Lincoln (one John de la Pole),
King Richard's named successor – on the whole
A nasty bit of work; another such
Was the exiled Lord Lovell, who owed much
To Henry's mercy. An earlier plot,
Led by Lovell, had collapsed. Do you know what?
He was pardoned: exiled, but at liberty
To re-offend. Which he did! Pure treachery.
And, financed by Margaret of Burgundy,
Were hordes of mercenaries from Germany.
She was the sister of Edward the Fourth
And still enjoyed strong backing in the north –
Bitter, resentful, and a regular thorn
In Henry's side, who wished she'd never been born.

The Tudors

The King's army faced down the rebels at Stoke.
Had the enemy triumphed, then (at a stroke)
The Tudor dynasty would have breathed its last.
The whole of history would have been recast.
No Henry the Eighth! No Gloriana!
No Francis Drake! No Spanish Armada!

Henry took matters in his stride that day.
As opposition seemed to melt away,
De la Pole was slain, others disappeared,
Yet the King's revenge was not as some feared.

A man of even temper and vision,
Henry even thought to make provision
For little Lambert Simnel. The poor lad –
A dupe, a mere victim, and far from bad –
Was despatched by the King, with a wry smile,
To the royal kitchens. Meek and servile,
He slaved away for a year and a day
On iron rations and very low pay.
But when Simnel died in his sixty-first year
He was royal falconer. That's some career!

Perkin Warbeck

The second Pretender to Henry's throne
Was Perkin Warbeck, another unknown.
Tall and handsome (in a weak kind of way),
Warbeck was 'talent-spotted' one fine day,
By Yorkists, strolling in the streets of Cork.
Something distinctive in the young man's walk
Attracted their notice. Warbeck was green,
Easily flattered and just seventeen.
How they persuaded him, Lord alone knows,
Yet within minutes, so the story goes,
They'd convinced him he was the youngest son
Of Edward the Fourth, whom everyone
Knew had been murdered by Richard the Third,
In the Tower. If that sounds too absurd,
It was. But Warbeck's impersonation
Was more than a passing irritation.
If Edward's true son and heir were alive,
Henry Tudor would struggle to survive.

Most of Warbeck's backing came from abroad
And this the watchful King could ill afford.
Avoiding warfare was a central plank
Of Tudor policy. This mountebank
Enjoyed, variously, the strong support
Of France and Austria, and even thought
To offer the Emperor, then and there,
The succession, should he die with no heir.
Ireland and Scotland got in on the act –
The Netherlands, even, and that's a fact.
Margaret of Burgundy, poor old soul,
Coached her 'nephew' in his imposter's role.
For six years Warbeck rattled around abroad.
Henry waited, pretending to be bored.

In 1497, at long last,   **1497**
Warbeck launched his attack. Henry moved fast.

6

The rebels surrendered without a fight –
Perkin himself did, at least. At midnight,
The Pretender abandoned his forces
(6,000 Cornish troops), stole some horses,
And rode to seek forgiveness of the King.
His cynicism was quite sickening.
Most expected Warbeck's execution,
Quick and clean – the obvious solution.
Henry Tudor was made of better stuff.
Although after six years he'd had enough,
In his darker days he'd learnt to forgive.
So he let the vain interloper live.
Warbeck was kept a prisoner at Court,
No longer a threat – or so the King thought.

The fool, however, tried to escape. Twice.
The penalty now wasn't quite so nice.
In 1499 he was hanged, and –   **1499**
In a move less easy to understand –
The Earl of Warwick was sent to the block,
On trumped-up charges. This was quite a shock.
A male descendent of Edward the Third,
He posed a real risk and, in a word,
He had to go. It was just to 'make sure'.
Now Henry was safe and England secure.

Prince Arthur

More important still was the succession.
Within eighteen months of his accession,
Henry's Queen gave birth to a baby son,
Prince Arthur, followed by a second one,
Henry, five years later (a kind of spare).
There was wild rejoicing everywhere.
Two healthy young daughters there were, of course:
Margaret and Mary. The driving force,
However, in this dynasty was male.
A Tudor Queen of England? Bound to fail.

Politics, finance and trade

Thus the new King entrenched his position.
Let us then examine the condition
Of the kingdom he came to inherit.
Henry won the crown by force, not merit,
So had to prove his worth and prove it fast.
England's flag, as it were, stood at half-mast:
Demoralised by long decades of war
With, for all men knew, many more in store;
Still plague-ridden; the treasury bankrupt;
Split by factions; the government corrupt;
Religious laxness and impiety;
A sick, dysfunctional society.

The Crown was weak. Its return to good health
Hinged on the accumulation of wealth.
Over-dependence on the public purse
Meant conflict, instability – or worse.
Henry proved a first-rate businessman:
He never missed a trick. His reign began
With wholesale and widespread confiscation
Of Yorkist estates. The reclamation
Followed of all Crown lands (records survive,
Dating right back to 1455)
Over which royal control had been lost.
This, you can imagine, was at huge cost
To his over-mighty subjects. The King,
However, newly enriched, was laughing.

As income from royal estates increased,
So too did tariffs from trade, these, at least,
Once the new King had finally put paid
To tiresome foreign wars. Fortunes were made
(By himself and others) in cloth and wool,
With Henry at times less than merciful
Where tax evasion was concerned, or fraud.
In fact, he tightened up across the board

The Tudors

The whole system of forfeits, fees and fines,
Reforming them on more efficient lines.

Henry was no revolutionary:
The structure was already there, you see.
He took the old, rusting machinery
And buffed it up. He also, zealously,
Enforced the laws for keeping the King's peace,
Resulting in a most healthy increase
In revenue from judicial sources.
One of Henry's special hobbyhorses
Was the freeing from intimidation
Of juries. Before long the whole nation
Applauded the wisdom of these measures.

One of an historian's chief pleasures
Is recording political success.
Henry the Seventh, I have to confess,
Was a model and an inspiration,
Worthy of respect and admiration.

The King governed by consent, not by force.
He never slept a wink at night, of course –
Ever diligent, watchful of all men,
Thrifty, cautious, and only now and then
Moved to anger. Tolerant to a T,
He won that rare, elusive prize: unity.

Henry hand-picked his chief ministers well,
A singular quality (truth to tell)
Shared by his two distinguished successors
Henry and Elizabeth, possessors
Both of similar wisdom and *finesse.*
King Henry the Seventh, nevertheless,
Was a 'hands-on' monarch. His eagle eye
Was gimlet-sharp and nothing passed him by.
Records of fines, taxes, rents from Crown land,
Were annotated in the King's own hand.

The accounts survive. You can take a look:
Thousands of notes in his little black book.

Henry, however, was no dictator –
Rather, a skilful conciliator.
He gave his subjects the clear impression
Of close involvement. His main concession
Was the King's Council, whose chosen members
Held 'discussions'. No one quite remembers
What they did. But Henry wooed, he flattered,
Made his mighty subjects feel they mattered.
Foreign affairs were discussed, and defence –
No one discouraged from giving offence;
But never fiscal policy, taxation,
Customs and excise, or land valuation.

Henry's well-anchored financial strength meant
Limited reliance on Parliament.
In his entire twenty-four-year-long reign
He summoned it just six times, and it's plain

The Tudors

No one thought this at all odd. Then again,
Nobody had any cause to complain.
Parliament doubled as a high court,
But other cases were routinely brought
Before the Star Chamber or the King's Bench.
This was adjudged no particular wrench:
Justice was swift, decisions were snappy;
If verdicts were fair, people were happy.

As for Parliament's law-making role,
I'd hazard a guess and say, on the whole,
This wasn't much needed in Henry's reign.
He was, as we've seen, inclined to refrain
From radical reform, and much preferred
Consolidation to change. If he erred
In this, so be it. His way was to pause,
Reflect, then act. He wanted few new laws.

Not that Parliament failed to defend,
Jealously, its ancient rights. To this end
It objected, in 1496,
When the King (in a rare financial fix)
Sought to raise money without its consent.
Parliament resisted, and this meant
Henry was obliged, the following year,
To summon a session. He had no fear
Of opposition. He got his supplies –
But only when he asked, and he was wise
To apply. Parliament in those days
Was still in its late medieval phase.
Lords spiritual and temporal sat
Before the monarch on his throne and that –
Give or take a few judges and others –
Was that: a band of privileged brothers.
The burghers from the boroughs and the squires,
The knights and other bigwigs from the shires,
Had no right of access. They sat apart,
With their own 'speaker' – all men of good heart,

But out of Parliament. In their prime,
The 'Commons', as they became, over time
Would supersede the 'Lords', even the King –
But that's years hence, by any reckoning.

Foreign affairs

In the early years of this good King's reign
Foreign affairs were a permanent bane.
With troubles enough at home, wars abroad
Were a luxury Henry could ill afford.

England was bogged down in a scrap with France –
A sterile compact with Spain, with no chance
Of success or reward. Against advice,
Henry sought peace, though not at any price.

At Étaples, in 1492,
He scored the perfect diplomatic *coup*.
Surrendering England's historic right
To *la terraine française*, without a fight,
He renounced all claims (except to Calais)
But made quite sure, before he walked away,
Of one concession from the enemy:
A compensatory indemnity
Of one hundred and sixty thousand pounds!
Unheroic, perhaps, but few had grounds
For doubting Henry's financial cunning.
As diplomatic triumphs go: stunning.

Problems with the Welsh Marches, which dated
Back centuries, were alleviated
By Henry Tudor's own Welsh ancestry.
Scottish disputes, too, became history –
Though this took quite some time. King James the Fourth,
Ever a brooding presence in the north,
Was brought in successfully from the cold
By the gift of Margaret (twelve years old),

Henry's daughter, in marriage. Odd ways
Kings had of solving disputes in those days.

This pre-arranged match had implications
For both these formerly scratchy nations,
Undreamt of when the treaty was agreed.
One Mary, Queen of Scots, (trouble indeed)
Was their granddaughter. We'll meet her anon.
But back to Henry – we need to get on.

Relations with the Netherlands improved.
They'd begun badly. The 'sting' was removed
Once the Warbeck affair had been settled.
Henry had been seriously nettled
By the strong succour the Low Countries gave
To this puffed-up, proud and dangerous knave.
However, the brisk trade in cloth and wool –
Vital in keeping England's coffers full –
Outweighed any sense of *pique* he might feel.
Relations, then, stayed on an even keel.
The *Intercursus Magnus* boosted trade
(That's a treaty), and huge fortunes were made.

Arthur's marriage... and death

Arthur, Henry's heir and favourite son,
Was married with pomp in 1501.   **1501**
His bride was Catherine, from Aragon,
Of Spanish blood – wooed and royally won.
The Prince, at fifteen, was a lucky boy.
The whole population went wild with joy:
Jousting and feasting, pageantry and plays,
Festivities lasting a full ten days.

The Tudor dynasty had come of age.
The succession was secure. Yet off-stage,
Waiting in the wings, lurked Death. Five months on,
Young Arthur breathed his last. Alas, he was gone.

Prince Henry

Henry the Seventh had a second son,
His namesake. Once the funeral was done,
He had a bright idea. Hating waste,
He proposed (hardly in the best of taste)
That Henry marry the grieving widow.
Gift of a doting dad? I don't think so!
On old Henry's mind, you can bet your life,
Was the dowry that came with Arthur's wife:
Two hundred thousand gold crowns. Pay them back?
You must be joking… Onto the attack…

Poor little Henry didn't have a hope.
He did as he was told. Next stop: the Pope.

Julius the Second's dispensation
Was requisite for the celebration,
If lawful, of this second marriage.
Henry couldn't risk the miscarriage –
Legal, moral, ecclesiastical –
Of his plan. It may sound fantastical,
But Julius gave his ready consent.

For Henry this coveted ruling meant
He kept his money. It meant more, of course:
Years later, a certain royal divorce
(The need for which was no real mystery)
Changed the whole course of modern history.

The King rarely meddled in Church matters.
His son's reign saw relations in tatters,
But Henry *père* left the Church well alone.
Deference to Rome was the cornerstone
Of his design. He risked the odd reform,
But change was limited and not the norm.

King Henry's character

Henry was a man of some piety,
Virtue, modesty and sobriety.
Astute, ascetic (plain for all to see),
He left a most impressive legacy:
A kingdom at peace, at home and abroad –
Solvent, united, its future assured.

Pictures suggest a frail man wracked with care,
With over-anxious eyes and thinning hair.
On display in the Portrait Gallery –
Go take a look, it's there for all to see –
Is a painting by Holbein the Younger.
It depicts Henry the Eighth – warmonger
And (excuse the expression) whoremonger –
Sturdy and stout (his pretence at vigour).
In the background there's a lesser figure,
In a long ermine robe, slender and tall.
At first you hardly notice him at all.
That's appropriate. Few people have heard
Of Henry the Seventh, and that's absurd.
Single-handed, he rescued the nation –
That's no word of an exaggeration.
In my opinion, at any rate,
He's not just 'the Seventh', but Henry 'the Great'.

On April the 21st, 1509,   **1509**
After several months of steady decline,
Henry breathed his last. He was fifty-two.
A gentle, noble King. My liege – adieu.

HENRY THE EIGHTH (1509 – 1547)

His second son succeeded. Arthur dead,
England was saddled with Henry instead.
King Henry the Eighth, aged barely eighteen,
Was set, within weeks, to marry his Queen.

Rhyming History

Catherine, Arthur's widow, had waited
Seven long years, a delay she'd hated.
Senior to her husband by six years,
This sad alliance was to end in tears.

But for now there was wild jubilation:
A royal wedding, a coronation,

A handsome young King in the prime of life,
Virile and strong, with a fine Spanish wife.

Henry was all that his father was not.
His subjects decided (a fickle lot)
They suddenly valued youth over age.
Old Henry hadn't been keen to engage,

The Tudors

As we've seen, in needless and costly wars.
Henry (the son) hardly bothered to pause
Before ganging up with the King of Spain
(His father-in-law) against France. His reign
Began as it would end, with French campaigns –
Wasteful, expensive, and with no real gains.

Henry thought rather a lot of himself.
Where his father carefully amassed wealth,
He spent it. Where his father was modest,
He'd show off in an archery contest.

Henry the Seventh had been a poor shot,
An 'indoor man'. Henry the Eighth was not.
Broad-shouldered, muscular and athletic,
His self-regard was frankly pathetic.

Rhyming History

In his own eyes Henry could do no wrong –
All very well when the country's 'on song',
But over time, as the going got tough,
This self-indulgent tyrant cut up rough:
A despot, no less – a vain autocrat.
As surely as his muscle turned to fat,
Men saw that they'd won a pig in a poke.
Henry's rollercoaster reign was no joke.

Back to the plot. Two swift executions
Occurred early on, easy solutions
To a non-existent problem. Treason
Was the charge levied, for no good reason,
Against Empson and Dudley. The scaffold
Was their unwarranted fate. Their heads rolled
Because their duties under the old King –
Fiscal enforcement (to my reckoning
Vital functions of government) – gave rise
To resentment and were (surprise, surprise)
Widely unpopular. The King smelt blood.
By choosing two victims whose names were mud,
He won an easy popularity
And acquired the taste, as soon we shall see,
For 'judicial' executions. Two wives,
For instance, out of the six, lost their lives
On the block – and ministers by the score,
Like Thomas Cromwell and Sir Thomas More.

Foreign affairs

King Ferdinand of Spain, father-in-law
To the new King, urged him to go to war.
The French had recently upset the Pope,
And Henry, a staunch Papist, lived in hope
Of recreating that chivalric age
When warfare and heroics were all the rage.
Though Agincourt was ancient history,
Henry relived that famous victory,

Albeit in his dreams. At any rate,
Only conquest of France would satiate
His naked, adolescent ambition.

By 1512 this was the position: **1512**
England and Spain, together with the Pope,
Were at war with France. For Henry, the scope
Of this conflict took in Scotland, back door
To his kingdom, and sure to join the war
On the French side, for they were old allies.
Parliament, it came as no surprise,
Voted all the necessary supplies.
I say 'no surprise' because the nation
Thirsted for some foreign confrontation.
There hadn't been a decent war for years.
With alleluias ringing in his ears,
Off went Henry on his quest for glory.
The truth, though, was a different story.

The Spanish strategy was underhand
And unreliable. Success on land
Eluded the King, though he did his best.
Then, in April 1513, at Brest,   **1513**
His navy suffered a major defeat
And, to make Henry's agony complete,
Ferdinand abandoned England and Rome.

A lesser leader might have limped off home
But Henry, livid with the King of Spain,
Marched into France and, like a hurricane,
Scored at Spurs a most splendid victory.
To say 'success' were contradictory:
Though the King returned home to great applause,
Those men who troubled to take time to pause –
Given that the gains were not extensive,
And the campaign was hugely expensive –
Knew that the King was on the defensive.

Rhyming History

While Henry was muddling through in France,
The Scots were leading him a merry dance,
Just as he'd feared. From his fiefdom up north,
Henry's own brother-in-law, James the Fourth,
Attacked. On the 7th of September –
A date the Scots will ever remember –
At Flodden Edge, King James himself was slain.

Figures are difficult to ascertain,
But over 10,000 men fell that day –
A foul and bloody massacre, they say –
Including Scotland's governing *élite*.
Earls, lords and bishops went down to defeat.

This most satisfactory solution
Was matched by a surprising conclusion
(Temporary, at least) to the French spat.
Spain had duped Henry. He didn't like that,
And so resolved to go on the attack.

Acting alone, behind Ferdinand's back,
Henry negotiated terms with France.
Spotting an opening, he seized his chance.
The new Pope, Leo the Tenth, much preferred
Peace to war – or so young Henry had heard.
Keen not to fall foul of Rome (though read on),
He made overtures to France, whereupon
A treaty was signed in 1514.   **1514**

The main provision sounds faintly obscene:
Henry's kid sister, Mary, became Queen
To the decrepit King Louis the Twelfth.
Henry was only thinking of himself.
Sundry French towns became Henry's, whose wealth
Increased accordingly; and a pension;
And more clauses too boring to mention.

Cardinal Wolsey

Now's time to introduce a new figure.
In influence there was no man bigger
Than Cardinal Wolsey. Ditto his girth.

Son of a butcher and of humble birth,
Thomas Wolsey was the King's right-hand man
For some fourteen years. His career began
As chaplain to the old King, under whom
He quickly made his mark. We may assume
That his talent and his reputation
Earned him, in the new administration,
His place on the Council. Over five years,
From 1509, with blood, sweat and tears,
Wolsey laboured twenty-four hours a day –
Often when the young King was out at play –
To establish his power. The French war
Gave him the break he looked for. Wolsey bore,

Rhyming History

On his great shoulders, the entire burden
Of equipping Henry's troops. His guerdon
(Or reward) for his success in this field
Was the King's high favour. Wolsey would yield
To no man in his quest for wealth and fame.
By 1514 he had made his name.

Consecrated as Archbishop of York,
He was on his way. There was even talk,
Among sycophants, of 'Wolsey for Pope',
Though Thomas, quite frankly, hadn't a hope.

Cardinal, however, he did become
The following year, which horrified some;   **1515**
Papal legate for life in '24;
And bishoprics and abbeys by the score:
Winchester, by far the wealthiest see;
St. Albans, the richest abbey. The key,
It seems, to his influence resided
In his iron self-will. He presided
Over a craven Council, who were cowed
By his bullying and bombast. Men bowed
Before him for fear of losing their place,
While Wolsey himself, an utter disgrace,
Feathered his nest, fathered bastards, took bribes
And bled the country dry. No one subscribes
To the notion (well, not any longer)
That the King was ignorant. The stronger
The dreadful Cardinal became, the more
Time Henry had for hunting, and the odd whore.
Government, frankly, was rather a bore.
Besides, what else were Lord Chancellors for?

So what did Wolsey actually do?
Sorry, gentle reader, over to you –
For I, to be honest, haven't a clue.
What of foreign affairs? A quick romp through...

The Tudors

The treaty of 1514 broke down
When Louis the Twelfth died, and the French crown
Passed to Francis the First. He preferred war
On all fronts. Wolsey and Henry were sure
He'd be bound to stir up fresh discontent
In Scotland. Indeed, this was his intent:
Francis ousted Margaret, Queen Regent
To the infant King James. Henry, hell-bent
On revenge, knew exactly what to do,
But he lacked the resources. What was new
Was the fresh vigour of Francis the First –
His youth, his good looks. Henry could have burst
With envy. Until the day the King died,
Francis remained a thorn in Henry's side.

France's aspirations were serious
In Italy, and deleterious,
In Wolsey's view, to Henry's position.
The King's fragile financial condition
Meant relegation to a lesser league,
But Wolsey ignored this. He loved intrigue.

Francis overran northern Italy.
Wolsey feared for the Pope. He bitterly
Resented the French force, or so he said,
And Henry gave his ready go-ahead
To pay secret subsidies to the Swiss
And Emperor Maximilian, this
Designed to encourage them to attack
The French. But the Emperor had the knack
Of double-dealing. He kept the money,
And did nothing! This might have been funny
Had Wolsey stopped there – but he was still keen
To play 'king pin'. When (in 1516)   **1516**
King Ferdinand of Spain finally died
(Succeeded by Archduke Charles), Wolsey tried
To twist Maximilian's arm again,
Exhorting him to renounce ties with Spain –

Rhyming History

Which had just signed a peace treaty with France!
Engagement in this diplomatic dance
Blew up in Wolsey's face. So very green,
This pompous, self-important go-between
Threw more money at his 'ally' (the clot),
Who broke his word and Wolsey lost the lot.

Still he refused to give up. France and Spain
Soon fell out and he was at it again.
Both leaders, Archduke Charles and King Francis,
Wooed Wolsey. Suddenly the stage was his.
Hobnobbing first with one, then the other,
He was in his element. Oh, brother –
Did he milk it! Over a year it took,
And Wolsey played his new role by the book.

He put together a grand alliance –   **1518**
England, Spain, the Pope, the Emperor, France –
All against the Turk. Buy that if you will.
The pact survived for just four months until
1519, when the Emperor died.   **1519**
The whole edifice collapsed. Wolsey tried
To urge Henry to stand for election.
The King, anticipating rejection,
Wisely backed off and the contest was won
By Charles, Maximilian's own grandson.

Emperor Charles the Fifth enjoyed, of course,
Massive prestige. No comparable force
Could match him excepting, possibly, France.
Henry was weak and didn't stand a chance,
Yet Charles and Francis both badly needed
His support. The Emperor succeeded
In securing Wolsey's backing. The Pope
Was still harassed by France. So, in the hope
(Ha!) of winning the papacy, Wolsey
Threw in his lot with Charles the Fifth. You see,
He was focused solely on Number One.

Despite this Anglo-Spanish pact, some fun
Was had at the Field of the Cloth of Gold.   **1520**
Francis, apparently, hadn't been told
Of Wolsey's backstairs deal with Spain. He came,
In good faith, to Calais to make his name
By jousting in a splendid tournament
With his 'friend' the English King. What this meant,
Though, was that all proceeded as before:
Henry played ball, while Wolsey planned for war.

Wolsey banked on the Emperor's support
When Leo the Tenth died. This came to naught.
Charles treated the Cardinal like a pawn.
Still, Wolsey ignored the Emperor's scorn
And goaded Henry into war with France.
Funds were low; Parliament looked askance
At voting supplies. Increased taxation
Proved most unpopular, and stagnation
In trade was blamed on the futile French wars.
Indeed, Wolsey's policies were the cause

Rhyming History

Of near-riots, in 1524,   **1524**
Against exorbitant taxes. The war
Then took a strange turn. The French were routed
By Charles in Italy and few doubted
The Emperor's advantage. However,
He abandoned Wolsey. Boxing clever
(So he thought), the Cardinal concluded
Peace with France! Now totally deluded
(Mad, some might say), Wolsey, in '26,   **1526**
Signed the Treaty of Cognac, a quick fix
If ever there was one. The dominance
Of Charles the Fifth was now countered by France,
England and the Pope. Pure self-interest
On Thomas's part, it must be confessed,
Was his leading motive. Still in a huff
At Charles the Emperor's papal rebuff,
Most of the Cardinal's prerequisites –
Backhanders, bribes, perks and side-benefits –
Were satisfied by the pact at Cognac,
Signed, as usual, behind the King's back.

Wolsey's strategy backfired yet again.
When Charles' armies plundered Rome, it was plain
That the Cognac treaty was a lost cause.

One of the Cardinal's most tragic flaws
Was his blind self-belief, but when the Pope
Was taken captive, he abandoned hope
(Even he) of setting matters to rights.
Already he was having sleepless nights
Over the King's 'great matter', his divorce
From Catherine, the hapless Queen. Of course,
All were aware the Pope alone could grant
Dispensation. But the Queen was Charles' aunt,
And the Pope was his prisoner. Oh, dear!
No wonder Wolsey felt a little queer.
So, he declared war. The country refused:
The people by now felt roundly abused.

The Tudors

Pope Clement the Seventh then turned the screw
By treating with Charles. What else could he do?
And the final blow: France made peace with Spain!
The Cardinal bounced back, time and again,
But not now. He'd blundered, and he knew it.
He'd had one final chance, and he blew it.

Wolsey was Chancellor for fourteen years.
They say that all political careers
End in failure. He had zero success
In foreign affairs. That too, more or less,
Was his record in domestic matters.
On leaving office, his life in tatters,
What in fact had the Cardinal achieved?
If the books I've read are to be believed,
Precious little. Economics, I fear,
Were a weakness. Thomas had no idea
Of sound finance, fiscal restraints, or trade.
His fellow councillors were of low grade,
All yes-men, so the administration
Devolved on him, with a concentration
Of power in his hands and his alone.

Wolsey, moreover, was the cornerstone
Of Church and State. As we've already seen,
Clerical abuses were quite obscene.
Thomas had no programme for Church reform,
No strategy. Corruption was the norm:
Simony, nepotism, bribery,
Pluralism and immorality –
Widespread, unchecked and plain for all to see,
With Wolsey as the grand epitome.
Small wonder the Church had such a bad name.
Henry was devout, but when the time came
To break away from Rome, there's little doubt
Some folk might well have been content without
A Church at all! The rotten Cardinal
Contributed, by his conduct and fall,

Rhyming History

To the easy acceptance by the nation
(And I mean this) of Henry's Reformation.

One area where he does deserve credit –
Wolsey did do something right: there, I've said it –
Was in judicial affairs. His talent
For order and detail (so I've read) meant
A steady, progressive development
In the law of Chancery: wills, contract,
Property, land and trusts. Wolsey, in fact,
Reckoned no man to be above the law –
No irony intended. Rich and poor
Were equally entitled, for their sins,
To justice. His own humble origins
Were surfacing, perhaps – his vanity
Eclipsed, for once, by some humanity.

The King's divorce

So, then, to the great matter of the divorce,
A drama which radically changed the course
Of post-medieval history, at home
And abroad. The historic break with Rome
Was precipitated by the King's need
To ditch Catherine. But many a seed
Had already been sown. The Church was weak,
Senior clergy a self-serving *clique*.

Church property accounted for huge wealth.
The laity eyed this up for itself.
Church privilege was widely resented.
'Benefit of Clergy' represented
The worst of these abuses. Any priest
Could escape criminal sanctions, at least
As a consequence of his first offence –
That's whether or not he had a defence!
Also bitterly disliked were the fees
Imposed by the Church authorities. These

The Tudors

Included payments due upon probate,
Mortuary tax and tithes. The same rate
Was levied alike on both rich and poor,
Which caused the Church to be hated the more.

The Pope's perceived remoteness was made worse
By Wolsey's *hauteur*. The Cardinal's 'curse'
Infected Rome by association.
His pride, self-regard and ostentation
Rubbed off on the Pope. So, come the big day
When choices came to be made, the King held sway –
Not some stuffy old pontiff living miles away.

These local considerations apart,
Tired of papal dominance, men took heart
From the 'new learning' which came from abroad.
Some yearned for novelty, some were plain bored,
But chaps like Erasmus from Rotterdam
Caught the mood of the times. An anagram
Of Erasmus is – wait for it – '*masseur*'.
I'm certain that I'm likely to incur
The contempt of purists, but this is apt.
Religious thinkers had been handicapped
By years of doctrinal orthodoxy –
Creeds subscribed to, as it were, by proxy –
But here was one for whom Bible reading
Supplanted the old tenets. By 'kneading'
(Or 'massaging') the religious conscience,
He urged scholars to dismiss as nonsense
The old medieval habits of thought.
Pure scriptural truth was what Erasmus sought.

Papal authority was undermined
By this so-called 'humanism'. We find
Adherents in John Colet, Thomas More
And hosts of others. The teaching was raw,
Novel and exciting and, it would seem,
Ushered in a new epoch. More extreme

Rhyming History

Was Martin Luther, another sound man.
The King, however, was never a fan.
Even after he had broken with the Pope
He stayed a good Catholic. He couldn't cope
With too much revolutionary stuff.
Erasmus was radical, fair enough,
But Martin Luther was a bridge too far.
When More was Chancellor (the rising star),
Luther was denounced. King Henry himself wrote
Anti-Lutheran tracts, which got the Pope's vote.
Dubbed 'Defender of the Faith' for his pains,
It did show at least that Henry had brains.

In *Leviticus* it is deemed a sin
To take your brother's wife. Queen Catherine
Was Arthur's widow. Henry, a scholar,
Was prepared to bet his bottom dollar
That Princess Mary was God's punishment.
Failure to father male issue meant
The biblical curse was being fulfilled:
No children. Henry the Eighth, proud, self-willed
And ruthless, demanded a son and heir.
To blame poor Catherine was hardly fair:
Still-births, miscarriages – she'd had a few,
But now the ill-used Queen, at forty-two,
Was past child-bearing age. She had to go.
Another factor, if you want to know,
Was this lady-in-waiting, Anne Boleyn,
Doe-eyed and flirtatious. Living in sin
With your own dear wife was one thing, surely,
But to hitch up with Anne, prematurely,
Would have made matters worse. I must confess,
The King was in a pretty dreadful mess.

It's now 1527 by the way. **1527**
Wolsey convened a special court, in May,
To establish a *prima facie* case,
So Clement the Seventh, with a good grace,

30

The Tudors

Could ponder the matter and, in due course,
Issue Henry with his royal divorce.

Whilst the King's 'marriage' was still valid,
Anne was prepared to wait, and wait she did.
The girl was certainly no fool. She knew
She'd no choice in the matter. Very few
Suspected that papal dispensation
Could possibly be withheld. The nation
Would welcome Anne Boleyn as their new Queen.
Henry, the bachelor he'd always been –
His union void *ab initio* –
Could marry whom he pleased. Those in the know
Expected Clement simply to say yes.
Not a straightforward case, though, I confess:
The ruling of Julius the Second
Was under scrutiny, and some reckoned
That no learned papal predecessor
Could be overruled by a successor.

Yet the authority of Holy Writ
Underpinned this case. Was any Pope fit
To deny the word of *Leviticus*?
To sanction this would be ridiculous –
So argued Wolsey and Henry's allies.

It should, however, come as no surprise
To learn that Clement didn't give a hoot
For theology. He was resolute
Against the King's divorce. And the reason?
Charles the Fifth had declared open season
On Rome, including all of Clement's lands.
The Pope, a pawn in the Emperor's hands,
No longer had an independent voice.
He'd do as he was told. He had no choice.
Charles was Catherine's nephew, as we've seen,
And the Spaniards, frankly, weren't that keen
To see the downfall of their tragic Queen.

Rhyming History

Wolsey was in despair. Henry required
A cast-iron outcome. The first son he sired
On Queen Anne would be the next Tudor King.
The legitimacy of their wedding
Must be open, proven and beyond doubt.
Papal blessing they could not do without.

But they surely weren't going to get it
And, though the Pope would come to regret it,
He was steadfast in his opposition.

Clement did make one odd proposition:
Legitimise Anne's children, one by one,
As they were born, then, if she had a son,
He could claim royal legitimacy!
Sending Catherine to a nunnery
Was the next faintly bizarre suggestion,
Designed to give Wolsey indigestion.
The Cardinal was caught in a cleft stick.
Anne Boleyn, personally, made him sick –
But he realised, to survive at all,
He needed the Pope, who wouldn't play ball.

The affair dragged on, beset with delays,
As a frantic Wolsey searched for new ways
To force the stubborn Clement back on side.

He failed. Specially undignified
Was the trial in which Henry, face to face
With Catherine, sought (to his lasting disgrace)
To prove her union with his brother
Had been consummated – she the mother
Of his own young daughter! This she denied.
Calm throughout, and serenely dignified,
The sad Queen commanded total respect
And, when the time came, as you might expect,
Accepted her fate as she knew she must.
Anne Boleyn outlived her – but only just.

Wolsey's fall

Poor Wolsey was at the end of his tether.
A born survivor, whatever the weather,
He'd run out of options. He was afraid.
The Cardinal – 'he who must be obeyed' –
Had incurred, and he knew it, the King's wrath.
Courtiers, councillors, men of the cloth,
Were quickly aware which way the wind blew
And deserted him in droves. They all knew
The fat Cardinal's time was up. His fall
Was absolute. Reputation was all.

He was finally arraigned for treason
In 1530, for no good reason.   **1530**
Fully aware of what his fate would be,
The final act of Wolsey's tragedy
Was a sad, lonely death. A long farewell
He bade to his greatness. So Wolsey fell.

Thomas Cromwell

It took another three long years before
The King got his divorce. Sir Thomas More,
The new Lord Chancellor, refused point blank
To interfere. Henry had cause to thank
Another Thomas for setting him free:
Thomas Cromwell. By 1533   **1533**
Cromwell was well entrenched. A man of steel,
He set about to bring the Pope to heel.

Ruthless and bold, the only solution,
Cromwell understood, was revolution.
Nothing short of a clean break with the Pope –
Divorce from Rome – was Henry's only hope.
The concept sounded simple, and it was.
Moreover, there was urgency because

Rhyming History

Anne Boleyn was with child, and September
Was her due date. Henry's son, remember,
Had to be legitimate. Time was tight,
And Cromwell knew he had to get it right.

The ground was well prepared. Parliament
Had been wooed for years, as Henry's intent
Had wisely been to cultivate, at home,
Strong allies in his struggle against Rome.
Cromwell favoured a clean break. However,
He understood (not just tough, but clever)
That the authority of statute law
Should serve to underpin reform. Therefore,
He drafted legislation (which was passed)
Of seminal import. He acted fast.

The Act of Appeals (1533)
Was the bedrock of reform. This, you see,
Abolished the Pope's sole right, at a stroke,
To adjudicate (no word of a joke)
Within the domestic jurisdiction
(As thus defined) of the King. The fiction
(As it now became) of papal status
Melted clean away, the apparatus
Of justice now belonging to the King.

As for the Queen, this only meant one thing:
Her time was up! Rome was simply by-passed.
Henry could marry Anne Boleyn at last.

Anne Boleyn

The wedding had already taken place!
She 'rounded', as the saying goes, 'apace' –
Hence the urgency. Though unexpected,
All due formalities were respected.
Archbishop Cranmer of Canterbury,
Deriving clerical authority

The Tudors

From the recent Act, convened a new court.
There wasn't a man who honestly thought
The poor Queen stood a chance and they were right.
Cranmer decreed, to Anne Boleyn's delight,
The 'second' marriage valid. All fears
For the succession were laid to rest. Tears
Were shed by wretched Catherine, of course.
She wasn't even granted a divorce –
She'd been living in sin! Never been Queen!
The moral implications were obscene.

Anne Boleyn became the toast of the town.
She played her cards well and she got the crown.

The Queen gave birth to a baby Princess,
Which caused the King not a little distress.
Henry, in fact, was extremely annoyed.
Three years Anne lasted, the union void:
The King had been married, so Cranmer decreed!
The role of a consort was simply to breed
And little Princesses weren't fit to succeed.

Anne failed to deliver, producing no son.
So wife Number Two followed wife Number One —
Into oblivion. Poor Anne lost her head.
Two down, four to go. But I'm running ahead…

The Church reform programme didn't end there.
Eyebrows were raised, but Henry didn't care.
Whether or not he was wholly aware
Of the full significance of the laws,
He allowed Cromwell, with barely a pause,
To introduce statute after statute
Until his dominance was absolute.
The King became the Church's Supreme Head:
That's what the Act of Supremacy said.

This Act was passed in 1534   **1534**
And, in the same session, another law —
The Act of Succession — put beyond doubt
The 'truth' that Henry could not do without.
Into statute went the confirmation
Of his 'divorce' and the affirmation
Of the 'legitimacy' of Queen Anne —
And her issue. Part of the master plan
Was an oath to the Act of Succession,
To be taken by all — no discretion.

The former Chancellor, Sir Thomas More,
Was willing to subscribe to any law
That guaranteed full legitimacy
To Queen Anne's children. But, more's the pity,
He couldn't look to God and swear the oath.
He, Thomas More, and Bishop Fisher both,
Had doggedly opposed the King's divorce,
And the schism with Rome. Their stand, perforce,
By definition implied denial
Of the status of the King. More's trial
Was a *cause célèbre*. The Treason Act
Outlawed the denial, by stated fact,

By deed or by word, of the name, title
Or dignity of the Queen and King – vital,
Of course, to Henry's colossal ego,
But sad indeed that Thomas had to go.
Rough justice and cruel persecution
Led to his and Fisher's execution.

Both lost their heads in summer '35   **1535**
And showed more guts than any man alive.

The Dissolution of the Monasteries

The Act against the Pope's Authority   **1536**
Won the expected large majority
When Cromwell, with Henry's commendation,
Secured, with minimal emendation,
Its passage through Parliament. By now,
Though, plans were afoot nearer home – and how!

Monks and abbots trembled in their boots.
Rumour had it they were in cahoots
With Rome. Most religious houses, true,
Had sworn the royal oath. In Henry's view,
However, any papal revival
Would start with the monks. The King's survival –
And that of the entire Reformation –
Required the seizure and the confiscation
Of all monastic lands. So Cromwell said –
And where King Henry followed, Cromwell led.
The power, verily, behind the throne,
This was his policy and his alone.

The Rome argument was a diversion.
Far more pertinent was the aversion
Felt towards the monasteries for years
By the laity. Cromwell, it appears,
Exploited the popular mood. Zealous
To a fault, he saw how very jealous

Men were of the monks' almost obscene wealth.
Royal funds, moreover, were in poor health:
This, to be blunt, was his foremost reason.
The declaration of open season
On the monasteries – 'dissolution' –
Was the perfect, tailor-made solution
To the King's worst nightmare. He was bankrupt.
Strictly speaking, it couldn't be corrupt
To seek to bail him out. But first things first.
Before the government could do its worst,
Cromwell commissioned a mammoth survey
In minutest detail (such was his way)
Of all Church estates across the nation.
This major feat of administration –
Called the *Valor Ecclesiasticus* –
Was achieved, with a minimum of fuss,
In just six months. Armed with valuations
And sundry dubious revelations
Of decadence, corruption and decay,
Cromwell's campaign soon got well under way.

In 1536 it all began.
Parliament united, to a man,
To approve the wholesale dissolution
Of each and every institution
Worth two hundred pounds *per annum* or less.
This was hypocrisy, I must confess,
On Cromwell's part. The transparent pretence
That only these were rotten made no sense.
He was testing the waters. Sensible,
Perhaps, but deeply reprehensible.

The buildings themselves were razed to the ground.
As for the monks, though, positions were found
In other houses. They even received
Pensions, if records are to be believed.
That they were treated with humanity
Comes as a surprise. The profanity,

Though, of the whole process did cause huge grief.
The crude destruction quite defies belief:
Libraries burnt, stained-glass windows smashed,
Manuscripts despoiled and paintings slashed.
Gold, silver and lead, all were melted down –
With every penny going to the Crown.

By 1540 the whole job was done.   **1540**
The greater institutions, one by one,
All succumbed to the same fate. Crown income
Rose by over one hundred thousand pounds –
That's *per annum* – providing ample grounds
For some modest self-congratulation
Among the King's men. Remuneration,
In the form of 'commission', I dare say,
(With the King's permission?) came Cromwell's way.

The enormous cost of war, however,
In the 1540s (far from clever:

Henry foolishly overplayed his hand)
Obliged the King to sell off half this land.
Within a decade two-thirds had been sold.
The noble folk who parted with their gold
Acquired with their estates, I would suggest,
A property-entrenched self-interest.
Should ever Papists try to stop the rot,
They'd lose the title to their lands – the lot!
This helps explain why Tudor society
Never quite warmed to Queen Mary's piety.

The Pilgrimage of Grace

Right in the midst of the dissolution
There occurred a mini-revolution.
The Pilgrimage of Grace convulsed the north.
The dissidents (Catholics and so forth)
Chiefly objected to Cromwell's power.
Robert Aske, the hero of the hour,
Led hordes of insurgents, all excited
By injustice, but hardly united
When it came to a single objective.
The main source of the rebels' invective
Was a Catholic-inspired revulsion
For Cromwell's policies: the expulsion
Of the abbots; the widespread destruction
Of the abbeys; the wholesale reduction
Of local governance; the enclosures;
Raised rents; even malicious disclosures
Of witchcraft and mischief – a rigmarole
Of hearsay and rumour. Henry's control
For some time looked dangerously shaky.

The rebels' commitment, though, was flaky,
Loose-knit and diffuse. Robert Aske was tried –
Fairly or not I'll leave you to decide –
And, with the ringleaders, executed.
Others had their sentences commuted.

The Tudors

This policy proved highly effective.
Cromwell and the King were quite selective:
Execute an abbot! Perfect excuse
To shut down the abbey! Call it abuse,
Corruption, cynicism – what you will.
Perhaps it simply gave Henry a thrill.

The Pilgrimage of Grace was soon snuffed out
And this contributed, without a doubt,
To the strengthening of the King's position –
The quelling, too, of Papist opposition.

Also, Henry's replacement of the Pope
As Head of the Church in England gave hope
To the strong anti-Catholic faction.
Protestants derived rich satisfaction
From the King's great reforms – Lutherans too.
One thing, though, that Henry could never do
Was renounce his Catholic roots. He still
Stuck with the old beliefs, for good or ill,
And held the balance, with consummate skill,
Between opposing faiths. Cromwell it was
Who bore the main brunt, and this all because
He dreaded Catholic threats from abroad.
After Wolsey, Henry was frankly bored
By the competing claims of France and Spain –
Alliances and so forth. Here again
Was Master Cromwell, urging him to make
Treaties here, treaties there… For Heaven's sake!
Who cared what other countries thought of Rome?
Besides, he'd far too much to do at home.

Anne Boleyn: an unhappy marriage.
The sad young Queen suffered miscarriage
After miscarriage. So, still no son.
The King only married, all said and done,
To father an heir – as simple as that.
Princess Elizabeth, snivelling brat,

Wasn't a boy. She wouldn't do at all.
So Henry contrived her poor mother's fall.
In 1536, early in May,
Less than four years after their wedding day,
Anne was arrested for adultery.
Her so-called trial was perfunctory.
Alleged to have had several lovers –
Among their number, one of her brothers –
Anne was executed, with five others,
Just ten days before Henry's third wedding.
That's some record, by any reckoning!

Jane Seymour

The lucky lady was one Jane Seymour.
She'd caught the King's lustful eye months before.
She must bear him a son, and she knew it.
Dying in childbirth, she nearly blew it –

The Tudors

But the infant survived. It was… a boy!
An heir at last! The people danced for joy!
Tragic for Henry to lose his new wife,
But baby Edward, the light of his life,
Furnished the King with justification
For all his past errors. Jubilation
Replaced despair as the English nation,
Sure at last of the continuation
Of the House of Tudor, simply went wild.
The wife of the King had borne a male child!

Anne of Cleves

The hunt was soon on for a replacement.
Cromwell, never one for self-effacement,
Set about this commission with a will.

Thomas, though, sadly showed limited skill
In the match-making department. His fear –
Deep-seated and increasing year by year –
Was that amity between France and Spain
Would isolate England. Time and again

Rhyming History

He warned the King of imminent danger.
Self-appointed 'marriage-arranger',
He sought a political alliance
With the Duke of Cleves – not in defiance,
Exactly, of the King, but he worked hard
To win Henry over. Cromwell's trump card
Was that Cleves had a sister (another Anne).

Cromwell was canny and cooked up a plan.
He passed around Anne's portrait. "Oh, how fair!"
They all enthused, "She's perfect!" – unaware
That Holbein had flattered the wench. Of course,
Poor German Annie was built like a horse.
The King was caught. The Fräulein was a fright.
This was apparent on very first sight.
Lumpen and plain, he called her a "fat mare" –
Out loud, in public. Such was his despair.

Their short marriage was celebrated,
But not (I've been assured) consummated.
The King never forgave Cromwell his shame.
Although a union only in name,
The affair made Henry a laughing stock.
Thomas Cromwell, his right-hand man, his rock,
Had blundered badly and was sent to the block.

Katherine Howard

Within sixteen days of the royal divorce,
This loyal servant of the Crown died. Of course,
The King remarried, and on the very day
That Thomas met his Maker. I have to say
That for bare-faced cheek that takes the biscuit.
And Wife Number Five? Who'd want to risk it? –
The Duke of Norfolk's niece, one Katherine,
Cousin (can you believe?) to Anne Boleyn.
Just eighteen months she lasted. No virgin,

44

The Tudors

They later alleged, on her wedding night,
Henry discovered that his heart's delight
Made herself 'available' (catch my drift?)
To the young men at court. She got short shrift
From the King, believe you me. Twice her age,
He'd been besotted with his Kate. His rage
Was terrible. They feared for his reason.

Katherine Howard was charged with treason
And lost her head in 1542.   **1542**
Henry took to his bed. Well, wouldn't you?

Catherine Parr

Now a cynical and dispirited man,
And martyr to a fierce temper, there began
The final, erratic phase of his long reign.
The old goat decided to marry again.
Another child bride would be going too far,
So this time he settled for Catherine Parr:

45

Rhyming History

Twice widowed, trustworthy and amiable –
To be honest, the best choice available.

A Protestant, but non-political,
Tolerant, discreet and uncritical,
She suited the old man down to the ground.
Some say her influence wasn't profound,
But Edward, Elizabeth and Mary –
None of whom shared a mother – though wary
At first, as step-children are apt to be,
Warmed to the Queen, whose sense of decency
And rectitude were plain for all to see.
She earned their respect and admiration
And took sole charge of their education.

The children loved Catherine, not just because
She was Queen, but for the character she was.
She outlived the King by only a year,
And when she died all England shed a tear.

The Tudors

War

Happy at home, Henry wanted a 'cause'.
Fond in his early youth of foreign wars,
His roving eye turned once again to France.
Spain offered support. He spotted his chance –
But first to Scotland. Secure the back door:
Useful advice before starting a war.

Scotland and France, traditional allies,
Posed a joint threat and this, in the old King's eyes,
Was the challenge. A strong Papist faction,
Backed by the French, still ruled Scotland. Action
Was thus launched against the unruly Scot
To oust the Papists and to stop the rot.

Between 1540 and '42
Honours were even. Then, out of the blue,
The English, outnumbered at Solway Moss,
Won a terrific victory. The loss
Was low, on both sides, in terms of men killed –
But the Scots, demoralised and weak-willed,
Were routed and surrendered by the score.
This was the high point in a futile war.

When James the Fifth of Scotland heard the news,
He keeled over and died! Henry could choose
From one of two straight options: invasion
Or diplomacy. On this occasion
He chose the latter, and few were surprised
When the Scottish Papists, destabilised
By Solway Moss, simply melted away.
French influence, it seemed, had had its day.

Henry was riding high, or so he thought.
A royal alliance was what he sought –
Between Mary of Scotland (a baby)
And the five-year-old Prince Edward. Maybe,

Rhyming History

Just maybe, this plan might have succeeded
Had the King paused for thought, and conceded
The Scots were likely to be less than keen
To cede their independence – and their Queen.

But Henry forced on the Scottish nation
His Treaty of Greenwich. Their frustration
Breathed new life into the Catholic faction,
Leading to a bloody counter-reaction –
Yet more slaughter, violence and terror,
Born of sheer stupidity and error.
For years after Henry the Eighth had gone,
His legacy of hatred lingered on.

The King was blind to the damage he'd done.
The Scottish campaign was as good as won,
In his eyes. Egotistical and vain –
With no Master Cromwell now to restrain
His folly – off on the warpath again
He went, this time to France. A pact with Spain
Was agreed and, in 1544,   **1544**
He lurched headlong into a new French war.

He saw himself still as a big hitter.
The truth was he'd been a good deal fitter.
He was old. Borne aloft on a litter –
Diseased and obese, he couldn't walk far –
He travelled to France in person. His star,
However, was rapidly on the wane.
These were the saddest days of Henry's reign.
He captured Boulogne. That was about it.
Charles the Fifth made peace with France. Bit by bit
The King was sidelined, but just wouldn't quit.
Spurred on by his forefathers' ambition
To be Lords of France (in his condition
Frankly laughable), he dug in his toes,
And resolved never to give up. Who knows
What his stubbornness cost? The *Mary Rose*

Was sunk in defence of the town. The war
Dragged on. It was more than two years before
Henry saw sense. In 1546 –

1546

Now in a terrible financial fix –
The King renounced his claim to France, all except
Boulogne. This he kept. His father would have wept;
Not at the concession – no, the whole campaign:
Wasteful, expensive, and money down the drain.

Indeed, the war bled England's coffers dry.
The cost of warfare had spiralled sky-high:
Inflation, of course, we'd call it today –
Ill-understood then. Be that as it may,
The Crown had to sell, to cover the cost,
A vast acreage of land. Thus was lost
The wealth garnered by the dissolution –
Regrettable, but a neat solution
To Henry's financial embarrassment.
It kept the land-owning classes content.
Instead of weakening his position,
It deflected any opposition

From those who'd been forced to bear the expense
Of the war through taxation. This made sense.

Henry's legacy

Henry, for all his faults, was very shrewd.
His methods could be forthright, even crude,
But when, aged fifty-five, the old man died,   **1547**
His legacy, it cannot be denied,
Was impressive. The monarchy was strong.

He made the rules up as he went along,
But he got results. The Reformation
Heralded the wholesale liberation
Of the Church from Rome. It began, of course,
Haphazardly, with the royal divorce.
Pragmatically Henry proceeded,
Supported by Cromwell, and succeeded
In an almost bloodless revolution.
"Every problem finds its solution,"
So opined Cromwell. Backed by force of law –
What else, he asked, was Parliament for? –
He stood by the King and saw through reform.

Confusion and bloodshed have been the norm
For revolutions down through the ages.
Volumes I could fill, pages and pages:
French, Russian, American and (read on)
English, to boot (although it's frowned upon
To mention it) – hundreds of thousands killed.
But under King Henry the Eighth, self-willed,
Ruthless and bloodthirsty though he could be,
Matters proceeded pretty peacefully –
Considering the Church, from top to toe,
Was riven with factions. Those in the know
Were prepared to afford Henry credit
For harmonious change – there, I've said it.

The Tudors

Folk sometimes also get the impression
That Henry was blinkered. The succession,
However, was safe. The Succession Act –
Mooted, it's true, with some measure of tact –
Secured the Tudor line of Kings and Queens.
First came Prince Edward (not yet in his teens),
Followed by Mary, then Elizabeth.
As Henry was drawing his dying breath,
He'd never have dreamt that his royal line
Would die out with Elizabeth. Aged nine,
Edward succeeded Henry to the throne.
If, on that sad day, the people had known
That each of the King's three offspring would die
Without issue… Well, at least he did try.
He did his best. Three children from six wives.
It goes to show, however hard one strives,
One cannot second-guess Fate. Henry expired
Clutching Cranmer's hand, lamented and admired.

EDWARD THE SIXTH (1547 – 1553)

Edward the Sixth was pious and haughty,
Precocious and a prig. Never naughty,
He was self-assured, formidably bright,
Protestant, proud and always in the right.
Sorry to speak so ill of the young chap,
But his wretched reign was one long mishap:
Five and a half years of muddle, and yet
Hardly his fault. The Duke of Somerset,
His uncle Edward Seymour, held the reins
As Lord Protector. Somerset took pains,
It seems, to put poor England on the rack
For three sorry years, before getting the sack.

Some will say his heart was in the right place.
Liberal by instinct (that's no disgrace),
He advanced the budding Protestant cause
By ending persecution. Henry's laws

On treason and heresy were repealed,
By which naïve move Somerset revealed
His lack of political grip. Dissent
Found a free voice, with reformers hell-bent
On changing the character of the nation,
Through religious debate and disputation.

Chantries were dissolved, where masses were said
For the souls of benefactors long since dead:
Purgatory was definitely 'out'.
The Catholic Mass would soon itself, no doubt,
Be the sole preserve of the ultra-devout.
What the chantry closures were really about
Was to generate extra funds for the state.
The Lord Protector's personal estate
In no small measure saw benefit too.
Corruption was rife. What else could he do?

The Prayer Book

Thomas Cranmer's *Book of Common Prayer*,
A work of scholarship beyond compare,
Appeared in 1549. This sought   **1549**
To conjure order from chaos. It brought,
Quite naturally, nothing of the sort.
Though Cranmer's work has stood the test of time,
Most in those days considered it a crime
To pray to the Lord in their mother tongue.
The Mass had always been spoken (or sung)
In Latin. That was what God expected.
No wonder folk so strongly objected.
But what caused the most pertinent comment
Was the Prayer Book's Protestant content.

Cranmer's new version was spectacular.
Perfectly crafted in the vernacular,
It combined a rare scriptural purity
With a rich, deep doctrinal maturity.

Somerset's policies

At the same time, England was on her knees
Economically. Prices, if you please,
Had more than doubled over the decade.
The people were angry. Tempers were frayed.
Peasant workers were thrown off the land
By the enclosures. Sheep, you understand,
Were cheaper to rear on open pasture.
The wool trade boomed, a total disaster
For your average peasant and his kind.
Landlords were greedy, and wilfully blind
To the needs of their tenants. Inflation,
Loss of livelihood, depopulation:
A lethal brew. Somerset, a mild man,
Took the side of the poor, and so began
A battle royal in Parliament.

Somerset signified his firm intent
To limit the enclosures. However,
The landlords would have none of it. Never.
The House of Commons was dominated
By their vested interest. They hated
The Protector, perceived friend of the poor,
And achieved their ends by passing a law
Subjecting vagrants to the exposure
Of savage new penalties. Enclosure,
Far from being curtailed, was left to thrive,
Profit and prosper. Into overdrive
Went the Lord Protector. Old Somerset
Was furious, but wasn't beaten yet.
He published, by open Proclamation,
The unequivocal condemnation
Of all enclosure. He did his level best,
But all he accomplished was civil unrest.

Peasants in Norfolk, led by Robert Ket,
Inspired, it's said, by our friend Somerset,

Rhyming History

Rose in their thousands in open revolt
Against the gentry. Ket launched an assault
On the City of Norwich, which he took.
For three critical weeks this had the look
Of dangerous revolution, its roots
Deep and well-watered. Ket was in cahoots,
Some thought, with Catholic Princess Mary.
They were wrong. What made Ket the more scary
Were his Protestant credentials. Orthodox,
This figure was something of a paradox:
A rebel who thought he had on his side
The Lord Protector. It can't be denied
That this put Somerset in a cleft stick.
He dithered, but what made him really sick
Was that the Earl of Warwick, his rival,
Routed Bob Ket. Somerset's survival
Hung in the balance. Perceived to be weak,
Outclassed by Warwick, his prospects were bleak.

The poor chap was put to yet another test
By a Catholic uprising in the west.
The old die-hards of Devon and Cornwall
Weren't fond of the new Prayer Book at all.
They rose up, determined to have their say.
What was so wrong with Latin, anyway?
Or the Pope, come to that? Lord Somerset
Yet again proved unequal to the threat.
Local leaders were left to take action
Against the rebels. Dissatisfaction
At Somerset's style of leadership spread –
And not without cause, it has to be said.

Fiascos abroad, it can't be denied,
Also played their part in his downward slide.
Somerset revived King Henry's old dream
Of Anglo-Scottish union. His scheme
Was to force through the Treaty of Greenwich –
The pact, you may remember, under which

The Tudors

The nine-year-old King was to be betrothed
To the wee Mary Stuart. The Scots loathed
The treaty. This didn't stop Somerset,
Who invaded. How stupid can you get?

An experienced soldier, his success
At the Battle of Pinkie meant far less
Than he imagined. The Scottish defeat –
Crushing, ignominious and complete –
Left the Protector gung-ho and upbeat.
His bloody triumph though was bittersweet.
He judged his single victory enough –
But Scots, we know, are made of sterner stuff.
Checking at a stroke Somerset's advance,
The French took Mary, Queen of Scots, to France.
Just like that! A gesture of defiance
Par excellence. The Scottish alliance
With France was stronger than ever before.
Somerset threatened. The French declared war,
Blockading Boulogne. Then (the final straw)
Came the announcement that the Queen of Scots
Would marry the Dauphin. Both were still tots,
But this 'union' of Scotland and France
Was fatal to Somerset. Mere mischance
It was not. He'd driven the Scottish Queen
Into the arms of the French. As we've seen,
His policies were rotten through and through,
Domestic and foreign. The palace *coup* –
Inevitable and long overdue –
Came in October 1549.

Somerset was arrested. So far, fine –
But his arch-rival, Warwick, now took charge.
While the Lord Protector remained at large,
By which I mean 'alive', his successor
Would never feel quite safe. A professor
Of the Catholic faith (observers believed),
The Protestant faction was mighty relieved

When Warwick routed the conservatives at Court
And identified himself with Protestant thought.
Ruthless and determined, he turned the boy King
Against his uncle. Somerset, poor old thing,
Was no real danger, but went to the block
On a trumped-up charge of treason – quite a shock!

The Duke of Northumberland

Warwick was out for himself, you understand.
Self-promoted to Duke of Northumberland,
He discharged Catholic bishops from their sees,
And exacted what he called 'economies' –
Effectively the payment of hefty fees –
Before appointing Protestants in their place.
This exploitation of church land (a disgrace)
Strengthened the Duke's own financial position,
While diluting the Catholic opposition.
The conservative bishops (Gardiner for one)
Languished in the Tower till Edward's day was done.

The new Prayer Book of 1552   **1552**
Was of an even stronger Protestant hue
Than the one of 1549. The King
Was pleased, the Reformation developing
Just as he wished. Cranmer was content too:
Long live King Edward! If only they knew...

Northumberland did accomplish some good.
He restored, as any governor should,
Better public order. Economies
Were made. Where Somerset had sought to please,
Northumberland spurned popularity,
Preferring to show solidarity
With the powerful and rich. This confirms
His political good sense. He made terms
With France by ceding Boulogne. He pulled out
Of Scotland. Some balked at this turnabout:

Shame and dishonour were how they saw it.
Northumberland didn't care. He bore it
Like a stoic, turning his attention
To domestic matters. I've made mention,
Above, of his greed and self-interest.
His sole concern was to feather his nest,
While keeping young Edward firmly on side.

The death of Edward

These plans imploded when the poor King died.
Edward was consumptive (we call it TB)
And succumbed in the summer of '53.   **1553**

Aware for some six months that he was dying,
What he found, as a Protestant, most trying
Was that Princess Mary, his named successor
And half-sister, was an ardent professor
Of Catholicism. Mary lived in hope
Of restoring the Church of Rome – and the Pope!

Death to Northumberland, that was for sure.
Pushing, as it were, at an open door,
He talked the King into setting aside
The will of Henry the Eighth: suicide,
Of course, but at least Northumberland tried.
The bare-faced cheek of it can't be denied.
Edward's two half-siblings were forthwith declared
Bastards! One wonders how Northumberland dared.
Both were by very nature of this decree
Disinherited. England should bow the knee,
Northumberland announced, to Lady Jane Grey,
Great-niece to the old King – oh, and by the way,
Just by chance his own teenage daughter-in-law!
When he mooted it first, Jane's jaw hit the floor.
A reluctant pawn in a dangerous game,
Poor Lady Jane acquired the dubious fame
Of reigning for just nine days. Edward's true heir,
Mary, fled to Framlingham in Norfolk where,
To widespread rejoicing, she was proclaimed Queen –
By right of succession. Deposed at sixteen,
Young Lady Jane was despatched to the Tower.
Northumberland, arch-villain of the hour,
Followed in her wake. Arraigned for high treason,
He lost his ugly head – with good reason.
Lady Jane Grey suffered a similar fate.
She said she was sorry, but sadly too late.

MARY TUDOR (1553 – 1558)

If Mary Tudor had played her cards right,
She might have gone far. Her prospects were bright.
Though plain, she was popular. More inclined
To mercy than vengeance, she was refined,
Gentle and intelligent. She sang well,
With a fine contralto voice, I hear tell.

But the people were in for a rude shock.
Queen Mary was of old Catholic stock.

The Tudors

Half-Spanish, her kinsmen came from abroad,
Which folk at home distrusted and abhorred.
England was in a state of mortal sin.
Henry the Eighth's 'divorce' from Catherine,
His first Queen, had been an aberration.
Her sole mission was to save the nation
By re-establishing the Church of Rome
As England's one true spiritual home.

After Edward, this came as a *volte-face*.
Mary continued to celebrate Mass,
In Latin, despite the Protestant laws.
Had the new Queen countenanced the shortest pause
Before turning the clock back to her grandfather's day,
She might just have succeeded. But that wasn't her way.

Thirty-seven years old when she came to the throne,
Mary determined (the decision was her own)
To marry into the Spanish nobility.
Displaying an astonishing ability

Rhyming History

To alienate her subjects, the new Queen chose
Her cousin Philip. This got up everyone's nose.
Philip was Emperor Charles the Fifth's son and heir.
The Council disapproved, but Mary didn't care.
Eleven years her junior, Philip was bland,
Plain and unprepossessing. On the other hand,
He was young and lusty. Mary craved for a child.
The House of Commons refused to be reconciled.
They feared England ending up in Spain's back pocket.
They hated the match, and did their best to block it.
Gardiner, now back in power, opposed it too.
The Queen ignored them. There was nothing they could do.
Indeed, displaying that Tudor 'orthodoxy' –
An iron will – she married Philip by proxy.

Dread of the growing Catholic ascendancy
And fear of possible Spanish dependency
Led, in '54, to a Protestant revolt.   **1554**
Under Sir Thomas Wyatt, a major assault
Was launched by some 3,000 angry men of Kent
On the City of London, the rebels hell-bent
On stopping the wedding and deposing the Queen.

They failed. Just. But what the rebellion did mean
Was that Parliament could no longer afford
To oppose the Queen's marriage. With one accord
They agreed that Mary could take Philip as King,
But should he outlive her, he'd lose everything –
His crown, his title, his privileges, the lot.
Protestants still saw this as a Catholic plot,
But when Philip survived her... Be that as it may,
It was game, set and match to Mary, I should say.
Oh, and Wyatt was executed, by the way.

It took the new Catholic Queen just two years
To undo her father's work. Protestant fears
Of Counter-reformation were justified.
In the early months Parliament defied

The Tudors

The Queen, managing to check, to some extent,
The pace of change. A stubborn Parliament
Refused to re-enact the heresy laws,
Repealed under Edward. The Catholic cause,
However, under Mary, was on a roll.
She and her new Archbishop, Cardinal Pole,
Were a formidable and determined team.
By November 1554, their dream
Of restored papal authority was fact.
The Act of Appeals, the Supremacy Act –
Both were repealed. The heresy laws came back,
As Pole, with a vengeance, went on the attack.
England was absolved from her sins by the Pope.
Burning of heretics was the only hope
Of cleansing the land of its Protestant ways.

Gardiner relished the task, ending his days
By consigning his old enemies – such names
As Ridley, Hooper and Latimer – to the flames.

Cranmer's fate

Thomas Cranmer had managed King Henry's divorce
From Queen Catherine of Aragon. She, of course,
Was Mary's mother. So there was little love lost –
As the poor Archbishop discovered to his cost –
Between Cranmer and the steadfast Catholic Queen.
Friend and adviser to Henry and, as we've seen,
To Protestant Edward, he was charged with treason
For plotting with Northumberland. The real reason,
It goes without saying, was his seminal role
In the English Reformation. Archbishop Pole,
His successor at Canterbury, and the Queen
Delayed his execution (I find this obscene)
Until the detested heresy laws were passed,
Which in 1555 happened, at long last.   **1555**
Cranmer, sixty-six, was tried as a heretic.
Then, having been found guilty (this bit makes me sick),

He was forced to recant. Cardinal Pole believed
This would weaken the Protestants, and was relieved
When this honest, erudite but confused old man
Finally offered his recantation. Pole's plan,
Endorsed by Mary, was to burn him anyway.
Resolved to the last to make their enemy pay,
They ordered Cranmer to make a public display
Of his recantation. So Thomas had his say.

At the stake he confounded the powers-that-be
By denouncing the Pope's usurped authority,
Whereupon he put his right hand into the flame:
"This hand," he cried, "hath offended. The very same
"Should be the first to be consumed." So Cranmer died.

News of his heroism travelled countrywide,
Faster than fire. It set back the Catholic cause
For generations. The dreaded heresy laws
Continued to be enforced. No lessons were learnt.
Over four years, some three hundred martyrs were burnt.

The end of Mary

'Bloody' Mary, then, the Queen came to be called.
Her hapless subjects were thoroughly appalled
When, following Charles the Fifth's abdication,
Philip became King of Spain. Concentration   **1556**
On home affairs drove the King from Mary's side,
And it didn't take Philip long to decide
That he much preferred the carefree, single life
To his frumpish, neurotic middle-aged wife.

However, England's worst fears were realised
When Spain declared war on France. Few were surprised
When the wretched Queen, abandoned and alone,
Threw in her lot with Spain. It's hard to condone
Her folly. Yet poor Mary was out of touch.
Still rumoured to love her husband very much,
And aching for a child, she staked everything
On pleasing the capricious, fickle Spanish King.

In June '57 England declared war: **1557**
Of the 'whys' and 'wherefores' nobody was sure.
The Queen commanded it, so it had to be.
Money was scarce, some funds raised illegally.
The final nail in Mary's coffin, some say,
Was when the French seized and overran Calais.
The war was in some senses the Queen's last chance
And, by losing England's last foothold in France,
She set the seal on her humiliation.
Booed off the stage by an ungrateful nation,
And drained of all vestige of personal pride,
She simply gave up the will to live, and died.   **1558**

The bells rang out to mark poor Mary's death,
While bonfires welcomed in Elizabeth.
The third new monarch, though, in twelve short years –
A woman, to boot. It would end in tears.

ELIZABETH THE FIRST (1558 – 1603)

Elizabeth the First was made of steel,
Yet still commanded popular appeal.
Striking of countenance, with flame-red hair,
She proved herself her father's one true heir.
Milksop Edward and the frightful Mary
Both left the populace rightly wary
Of the Tudors. Their new Queen, however,
Like old Henry, was not only clever –
Fluent in six languages (Spanish, Greek,
Flemish and French were four that she could speak) –
But she loved life. Pageantry she adored,
Hunting and dancing. Warfare she abhorred.

Here she differed from her father. The waste,
In money and men, was not to her taste.
This was closer to her grandfather's stance.
He, you may remember, withdrew from France –
A long-drawn-out war – as soon as he could,
Devoting himself, as a monarch should,
To peace at home and to the common good.

The Tudors

Henry the Seventh (you know I'm a fan)
By nature was a conservative man.
Elizabeth inherited this trait –
In spades. As Queen, she embodied the State.
She could be haughty, wilful, wayward, vain,
Yet she exhibited, throughout her reign,
The gift of caution. On her accession
She claimed she was "mere English". Possession
Of her crown, her life, her liberty, her throne,
She owed to the people, and to them alone.

Elizabeth, though, was nobody's fool.
Strong as an ox, and stubborn as a mule,
Her character was forged in early life.
Anne Boleyn, Henry the Eighth's second wife,
Was executed before Bess was three.
I should imagine (you may not agree)
That to know your mother's head was chopped off
By your own father might bring on (don't scoff)
Some kind of childhood trauma. Add to that
The fact that Henry never liked the brat.
When Bess was born he nearly had a fit:
An heir he needed, and this wasn't it!

Hardly the best of starts… Her step-mother
Was then charged with incest with her brother –
Queen Katherine, the fifth wife, beheaded
When Elizabeth was eight. She dreaded
The thought of matrimony. Small wonder.
Henry committed many a blunder
In his choice of wives. His daughter, with skill,
Played off suitor against suitor until,
In late middle age, she called it a day.
Hardly one to "love, honour and obey",
The Queen knew of course what she was doing.
Foreigners of all sorts came a-wooing.
She flirted, she flattered – strung them along.
The poor fools thought they mattered. They were wrong.

Rhyming History

During her childhood she was no stranger
To political intrigue. In danger,
Literally, of her life, the Princess –
About whom nobody seemed to care less –
Was twice under suspicion of treason.
In Edward the Sixth's reign, with good reason,
Thomas, Lord Seymour, was executed
For plotting (it's bit convoluted)
Against his brother, the Lord Protector,
With (as if anyone could suspect her)
Elizabeth's consent, barely sixteen –
And she to marry the rogue. Well, I mean…
Utter nonsense! If that had been believed,
Young Elizabeth would have been relieved,
By her brother, of her head, like as not.

The second, and far more serious, plot
Occurred during her sister Mary's reign.
Sir Thomas Wyatt rears his head again –
Remember him? Protestant fanatic,
And virulently anti-Catholic,
He marched on London to depose the Queen.
He failed, the foolish knight, and, as we've seen,
Answered for his treachery with his life.

Fearing further religion-fuelled strife,
Mary had her half-sister, next in line –
And Protestant, not an auspicious sign –
Arrested and imprisoned in the Tower:
Elizabeth's most dread and fearful hour.
The bastard issue of 'Queen' Anne Boleyn
Posed a dangerous threat. The poor girl's sin
Lay in her very birth. Urged to confess,
She gave her famous 'answer answerless' –
Astute, ambiguous and circumspect,
Canny, but truthful. As one might expect
Of one so sure of danger, she survived,
Against all odds, until her luck revived.

The Tudors

When Mary died, in 1558,
She left the country in a dreadful state.
Trading in wool was at an all-time low,
Which dealt the finances a bitter blow.

The Queen's own weakness, though, was most to blame.
The kingdom was governed, in all but name,
From abroad. England was in hock to Spain.
What funds there were had long gone down the drain
In the struggle with France – a futile war,
Entered into (I've no idea what for)
By Mary at Philip's instigation,
Her unctuous Spanish spouse. The nation
Was bankrupt, defenceless, and on its knees.

After Mary's death, Philip, if you please,
Entertained hopes of Elizabeth's hand –
His ex-half-sister-in-law! Understand
Elizabeth's position. The new Queen
Considered the mere thought of this obscene,
But, from the moment of her accession,
Parliament displayed an obsession
With the whole question of the succession.

Fortunately for her, in this instance,
Philip was widely disliked. Resistance
Was easy. Besides, the whole mad-cap scheme
Was a non-starter. The Catholic dream
Died with Mary. Englishmen hated Rome,
If not Catholicism. Their true home
Was Henry's Anglican Church. The nation
Had tired of the Counter-reformation.
Exiles, Protestants across the water,
Welcomed Henry the Eighth's second daughter
With arms wide open. The old King's divorce
Occasioned the break with Rome and, of course,
Elizabeth had been its issue. Well –
It wasn't all plain sailing, truth to tell.

Rhyming History

Religion

The main exiles from abroad were John Knox
(Hot-foot from Geneva) and Richard Cox
(From Frankfurt). Neither was to the Queen's taste:
Far too extreme. The creed they both embraced
(Knox more than Cox) was one that 'purified'
The Church of all things Roman. They decried
Papal authority. Well, that was fine:
So had old King Henry, all quite in line
With Elizabeth's instincts. Far further,
Though, these zealots went, and with a fervour
All quite alarming. Knox had lately been
Young Edward's chaplain. We've already seen
How, in that King's mercifully brief reign,
Protestantism took hold. It was plain,
Given the backing of Parliament,
Exactly what the Reformation meant:
A break not simply with Rome, but a lurch
Away from Catholicism. The Church
Established by Henry had, as its head,
Not the Pope in Rome, but the King instead.
Catholicism, though, remained the norm.
Edward altered that, in substance and form.

Mary, of course, restored the *status quo*:
The Pope, the Mass, the Roman Church. We know –
We've witnessed – how England bled. The wheel turned,
And many worthy heretics were burned.

Which way, men asked, would Elizabeth jump?
Thousands upon thousands would get the hump
Whatever the answer. She'd watched, she'd learnt,
As sister Mary got her fingers burnt.
The new Queen's preference (this is my guess)
Was the wholesale return (no more, no less)
To the Henrician Church with, at its head,
Herself in supreme command. With Mary dead,

The Tudors

The stage was set for a Catholic purge.
Elizabeth, however, felt no urge:
Just not her style. Caution was her watchword.
Pragmatism to conflict she preferred.
She demanded "no windows," she averred,
"Into men's souls" – which diehards thought absurd.

The Queen took care not to alienate
Philip of Spain. If the King threw his weight
With France against England, all would be lost.
So she kept him sweet, whatever the cost,
Humouring the old goat for twenty years.
Still, as we shall see, it ended in tears.
A major anti-Catholic campaign
Would, at this early stage, have been insane –
Even had she desired it. However,
Messrs. Cox and Knox were boxing clever.
Elizabeth's proposals made them sick.
Return to Henry's Church? Too Catholic!
The Queen, provoked and not a little miffed,
Prepared to give the Protestants short shrift
And yet... When Catholic bishops resigned,
En masse, where was Elizabeth to find
Replacements, if not from Protestant ranks?
Who'd be a Queen at twenty-five? No thanks!

This was no time for fire and fury.
Henry the Eighth had been judge and jury –
Arbiter in his own cause. Times had changed.
The make-up of Parliament now ranged
From the staunch Catholic right (the old guard)
To the new Puritan left. All fought hard
To be heard. Elizabeth understood
That it would do her royal cause no good
To ignore the emergent 'middle' voice
Of moderate Protestants. She'd no choice.
The Crown's influence had been on the wane
In matters religious since Edward's reign.

Rhyming History

His Prayer Books of 1549
And 1552 were all very fine,
But their authority, not just their enforcement,
Was underpinned by the will of Parliament.

Mary had found, to her intense irritation,
That she couldn't accomplish the restoration,
Without Parliamentary sanction, of the Pope.
Elizabeth, in short, hadn't the faintest hope
Of setting back the clock – at least in this respect.
She still put up a fair fight. You wouldn't expect
King Henry's daughter, with her awesome pedigree,
To do any less. In the first instance, you see,
Elizabeth resisted any Prayer Book.
The Protestants forced her to take a second look.

A new Act of Uniformity was needed,
The Prayer Book at its heart. The Queen conceded,
But ensured that the Act of 1559   **1559**
Was a compromise. Elizabeth drew the line
At certain provisions in the Cranmer version
Of 1552. She had an aversion
To several matters of form (quite minor now)
Concerning things like when to kneel and when to bow –
Far too remote to be of interest to us,
But apt, in those divisive times, to cause a fuss.

Elizabeth was signalling, to her credit,
Her latent Catholic streak. She never said it,
But the settlement to which she gave her assent,
On May the 8th, put paid to any argument
That she might subscribe to either of the extremes
Advocated by her siblings. Protestant dreams
Of a nascent Puritan state were laid to rest –
At least for now – while Elizabeth did her best
To see that Catholics who didn't toe the line
Were subject only to a very modest fine.

The Tudors

Henry the Eighth appointed himself, as we've seen,
Supreme Head of the Church. Elizabeth, as Queen
(A mere woman), couldn't be Head, so she became
Supreme Governor. Different only in name,
Some said. Not so. This title left her dependent,
As her father never was, on Parliament.
Henry had been, as it were, a 'Pope substitute' –
His powers, as such, virtually absolute.
But Elizabeth governed the Church from outside,
Its doctrine no longer hers alone to decide.

It's not quite true the Marian bishops 'resigned'.
They refused, to a man, to swear the oath designed
To test their allegiance, so found themselves deprived.
The brave souls fully expected they would be tried
And put to death. Yet Elizabeth spared their lives.
No record of vengeance or cruelty survives.
Their places were taken by Protestants like Cox,
Grindal and Jewel, Pilkington and Horne. Not Knox.
His elevation would have been a bridge too far.
Parker at Canterbury was the rising star.
Plucked straight from Cambridge,
                                as Thomas Cranmer had been,
Matthew Parker proved a huge asset to the Queen.
A moderate Protestant, scholarly, benign,
Cautious but tough, the new Archbishop held the line
Against the Puritans. He earned the gratitude
Of the Queen with his calm, no nonsense attitude.

No heretic suffered death (amazing but true)
Until twelve years into the new Queen's reign, all due
To Elizabeth's iron determination
To serve all her subjects. Excommunication
By Pope Pius the Fifth poisoned the atmosphere,
But had minimal effect. The climate of fear
Fuelled by Mary was a thing of the past.
Elizabeth's settlement was built to last.

Rhyming History

Scotland

By coincidence, a new religious order
Was poised to be established north of the border.
Mary (remember her?), the infant Scottish Queen,
Was despatched to France as a wee girl. At sixteen
She married the Dauphin, Francis, fourteen years old –
Son and heir to Henry the Second. Cruel, cold,
And scourge of the French Protestants, nevertheless
Henry did chalk up one significant success,
By concluding a treaty between Spain and France.
Celebrating the peace, he was hit by a lance –
Wielded by some mad Scottish Captain – in the head.
Ten days later this young flower of France lay dead.

Francis the Second succeeded, Mary his Queen:
Queen of two great nations, and barely seventeen.

So, who governed Scotland in Mary's long absence?
Her mother, naturally. It made perfect sense:
Mary of Guise ruled as Regent. Strong and able
(Though French), she contrived to keep the country stable
During her lifetime. But Scottish national pride
Was deeply offended. It couldn't be denied
That the French were an army of occupation –
Not just an insufferable situation
For the Scots, but harbouring all kinds of dangers
For the English. The two nations had been strangers
To peace for generations. England was now weak,
Defenceless and… Protestant. The outlook was bleak,
And Elizabeth knew it. But Philip of Spain,
Ever astute, knew that there'd be little to gain
(Should the Scots invade England) in a French empire
Of such range and strength. Philip's cardinal desire
Was to stay top dog. Should he choose to intervene
In an uncertain war against the English Queen,
France could turn up trumps. Ironically, his fears
Of Gallic strength kept Elizabeth safe for years.

The Tudors

To England, though, the Scots were an imminent threat.
Mary was Elizabeth's cousin, and dead set,
You can bet your life, on ousting the 'bastard' Queen.
Elizabeth's legitimacy, as we've seen,
Hinged on the legality of Henry's divorce
From his first Queen, Catherine. Catholics, of course,
Questioned its validity. Few, though, could deny
That Mary would succeed should Elizabeth die:
Henry the Seventh's daughter was her grandmother;
She had no male cousins living, and no brother.
Small wonder Protestants had such an obsession
With the Queen's marriage and with the succession.
Yet there were more than a few who saw in Mary
England's true Queen. This made Elizabeth wary,
And rightly so. A dangerous situation!

Scotland, under the yoke of French occupation,
Was still, on this account, a Catholic nation.
The Scots found a channel for their indignation
In the Protestant cause. Fired up with frustration,
And wrath, the self-styled 'Lords of the Congregation' –
Scottish nobles who abhorred their subjugation
To the hated French – mustered a numerous force
And rose up in revolt. Elizabeth, of course,
Watching from the sidelines, was loth to get involved.
This crucial issue, though, would never be resolved
(So argued William Cecil) unless the Queen
Gave succour to the insurgents. She wasn't keen.
Ever cautious, she finally gave her consent
To send a modest army north – and off it went.

The French were besieged at Leith. Their counterattack,
Swift and effective, drove the allied forces back.
Stalemate threatened. The French,
                              strong and well-organised,
Held the upper hand – just. Was the Queen ill-advised?
Then, as Fortune seemingly smiled on the French side,
Mary of Guise, their trump card, keeled over and died.

Rhyming History

Cecil, the English diplomat *par excellence*,
Set off for Scotland to negotiate with France.

The Treaty of Edinburgh was the outcome,
Signed in July 1560. It seemed to some   **1560**
That England's good fortune was too good to be true.
There's no denying that the Treaty was a *coup*:
All French forces were to leave Scotland at a stroke.
How was this achieved? Who knows! By mirrors and smoke,
For all I know. But Cecil's diplomatic skills
Were certainly to thank for curing Scottish ills.
The aforementioned Lords of the Congregation
Took charge, led by one Lethington, and the nation
Embraced the Protestant faith. The Reformation
Thus took root in Scotland, her humiliation
Throughout all those French Catholic years forgotten.
John Knox denounced the old religion as rotten.

Yes, though Knox was a thorn in Elizabeth's side,
It didn't take too long for the Queen to decide
That his crusading talents would be better served
North of the border. It was what Scotland deserved!

The Catholic threat was dormant, if not dead:
The Queen could sleep more soundly in her bed.

William Cecil, Lord Burghley

All down to Cecil. So, let's take a pause,
And consider this figure, the applause –
The accolades – still ringing in his ears.
He served Elizabeth for forty years.

William Cecil, later Lord Burghley,
Was marked out for royal service early.
In Henry the Eighth's court he was a page
(Of the wardrobe) at a very young age.
Brought up under Protestant influence,
To him the King's divorce made perfect sense.
Then he found favour with Lord Somerset,
Protector to the boy King Edward. Yet,
When Somerset fell, he served his rival,
Warwick. Heedless of his own survival,
He fell out with the Earl, the succession
The cause. Cecil opposed the accession
Of Lady Jane Grey, deserted Warwick
And, though Mary Tudor was Catholic,
He greeted her as England's lawful Queen.
Awkward, perhaps (well, no, it must have been),
But Cecil was a "very honest man"
(Mary's own words) and, as her reign began,
This vastly able, loyal bureaucrat,
This chief-of-staff and royal diplomat,
Withdrew from public life, and that was that…

…Until, of course, Elizabeth took charge.
The kingdom was bankrupt. Problems loomed large:
France; the Scottish Queen; religion; defence;
The Spanish question. It made perfect sense
To call for Cecil and, within three days,
The appointment was made. To overpraise

Rhyming History

The Queen's new Principal Secretary
Were impossible. Views, of course, vary
As to his character. Critics opined
That Cecil was too cautious, too inclined
To introspection, no innovator.
True, he was a fine administrator
And this, perhaps, blinded his detractors
To his genius. One of the factors
That marked him out – his aversion to risk –
Belied hidden strengths. Cecil could be brisk,
Forthright and pro-active. Set on a course,
He proved a strong and formidable force.
On occasion, his dogged persistence
Would trump the Queen's instinctive resistance.
The Scottish campaign was a case in point:
Cecil stood firm, and didn't disappoint.

He never sought to set the world ablaze,
But rather "walked invisible" – his phrase.
A master of discretion, the Queen's trust
He won with ease; her admiration – just!
For she was hard to please. He knew his place.

He only once experienced disgrace:
Elizabeth, in conscience, couldn't face
The awful truth of the execution
Of Mary, Queen of Scots. The 'solution'
Was 'managed' by Cecil (not before time).
Mary had committed the heinous crime
Of high treason – simply no doubt at all.
Her execution threatened Cecil's fall.
Elizabeth had long vowed she'd never,
Never sign the death warrant. However,
She did. Cecil was briefly her fall guy,
But soon bounced back – and I shall tell you why.
The Queen was nothing if not sensible
And, though nobody's indispensible,

The Tudors

Spain was re-equipping her fleet for war.
Cecil was needed as never before.

His influence runs like a golden thread
Through Elizabeth's reign. Cecil's cool head
Addressed the burning issues of the day.
He steered successfully a middle way
In foreign affairs between France and Spain
For nearly thirty years, until the strain
Of relations with Philip the Second
Finally defeated him. It's reckoned
That he built up, from a very low base,
England's finances. These were a disgrace.
Ditto the navy. Men were in despair:
Defences were in total disrepair.
It took years, but with imagination,
Leadership, hard graft and skill, the nation
Could face the full nautical force of Spain
And hold its head up proudly once again.

Peace at home helped, of course. Coincidence?
I don't think so. See what happened in France.
Torn apart by civil religious strife,
The French were weakened. You can bet your life
That Cecil and the Queen both understood
How wars at home would do no earthly good.
They saw that their religious settlement
Was foremost and fundamental. It meant,
In a nutshell, that England's energies
Were harnessed for progress. On the high seas,
Too, fortunes were being made. By degrees,
England discovered her national pride.
Hawkins, Gilbert and Raleigh sailed far and wide,
And Drake's global circumnavigation
Earned the respect of an entire nation.
Elizabeth, of course, was quite delighted:
On board the *Golden Hind*, Francis was knighted.

All down to Cecil too? Well, perhaps not –
But, present from Day Three, he stopped the rot.

The succession

One area where he had no success
Was the succession. The Queen feigned distress
Whenever the vexed question was mentioned.
Poor Cecil, civil and well-intentioned,
Sensed it was more than his career was worth
To press the point. A Prince of Tudor birth
(Or a Princess) depended on the Queen.
Elizabeth was very far from keen.
It's said, as early as the age of eight,
She settled firmly on the single state.

Maidenhood, in fact, became her trump card.
She played her hand with lofty disregard
For the feelings of the bizarre array
Of motley applicants who came her way.

Philip of Spain led the field, as we've seen.
Already widowed by one English Queen,
He tried Elizabeth, but wooed in vain.
Within a month the fool was back in Spain.
The Earl of Arran was a candidate,
A sickly Scot, and there was some debate
About one Eric of Sweden. His fate
Was sealed when they discovered he was mad.

Not all the aspirants were quite so bad:
The son of old Emperor Ferdinand,
Archduke Charles, a German, offered his hand.
He too was rebuffed. Few could understand
Elizabeth's reluctance. Her passion
Was fixed on a fine young man of fashion
Named Robert Dudley. Love unrequited?
Who knows? Cecil was far from delighted.

Dudley was a lightweight: handsome and vain —
And married. The Queen had little to gain
From such an affair. When Dudley's wife died
'In an accident', he hotly denied
Foreknowledge. Elizabeth's ardour cooled.
The Queen sniffed danger and was not to be fooled.

The crisis came in 1562.   **1562**
Elizabeth caused much hullabaloo
By catching smallpox. They diagnosed 'flu,
But no. By the time she took to her bed,
The Queen, they reckoned, was as good as dead;
Back on her feet in record time, of course —
She had the constitution of a horse.
But public confidence took a bad knock,
And Parliament suffered quite a shock.
Who'd have been crowned had Elizabeth died?
An heir must be found! It was time to decide!

In January 1563   **1563**
Parliament met and made history.
The House of Commons petitioned the Queen
To marry forthwith. Imagine the scene.
They professed themselves only curious
As to her choice. The Queen was furious.
Her marriage was a private affair —
No concern, as far as she was aware,
Of her Council, still less Parliament.

She was possibly right to that extent.
But the petition touched on the succession,
And this was within the Commons' discretion:
Henry the Eighth named all three of his heirs
By statute and had thereby, unawares,
Bound his successors. The King's precedent
Boosted the power of Parliament
And diluted that of the Crown. Livid,
Elizabeth stalled. And guess what she did?

Rhyming History

She fudged the issue of the succession
By walking away. She closed the session
By proroguing Parliament (just like that),
So turning all talk of marriage down flat.

Three years passed before a serious clash,
Triggered by a severe shortage of cash,
Occurred in October 1566.   **1566**

The Queen was in a rare financial fix,
Obliging her to recall Parliament.
The Commons registered their discontent
That their petition on the succession
Had still not been addressed. Their obsession
With the matter grew. They withheld supply
"Until her Majesty should make reply".
The Queen confessed no present plans to die,
But made this one concession. She might –
Indeed would – marry "when the time was right".
With this vague promise ringing in their ears,
The Commons "must be content". Three whole years
They'd waited, and for this! The final straw
Was Elizabeth's bid to close the door
On all further debate. Her bluff was called.
Faced once again with an *impasse,* she stalled.
The Commons' right to free speech was at stake.
The Queen, they sensed, had made a big mistake.

She knew it too, and with good grace backed down.
Battle between Parliament and Crown
Had been tentatively joined, then sidestepped –
A mere skirmish. Old Henry would have wept,
Felt undermined – nay, emasculated.
Elizabeth may have been deflated,
Humbled even – but humiliated?
No. For she still contrived to get her way.
She never married to her dying day,

Nor named a successor. Parliament,
Though, established its 'privilege'. This meant,
In essence, the principle of free speech –
Freedom in proceedings beyond the reach
Of the Crown. Many a battle royal
Was fought and much blood shed on English soil –
With one King, Charles the First, losing his head –
Before such freedoms were taken as read.
But the precious seeds were already being sown
Of Parliamentary Privilege – as it's still known.

Mary, Queen of Scots

The succession question was the more pressing
Owing to some items of news (distressing)
Touching the fortunes of the unmarried Queen.
We left Mary, Queen of Scots, aged seventeen,
In France – a recent bride, and now Queen Consort.

Brought up from the age of five in the French court,
Mary received, as befitted her station,
The very best classical education.

Rhyming History

French, of course, became her language of choice,
Though she was fluent in four. Her singing voice,
If tuneful, was slight; her dancing quite 'skilful';
Her temper wild and decidedly wilful.
This has to be said. What cannot be denied,
Though, was her great beauty. From her Tudor side
Came the flaming gold-red hair, the amber eyes,
The elegant, slender frame. It's no surprise
That she inherited from Mary of Guise –
The French side – her reputation as a tease,
A little flirt. That's to put it at its best.

Mary's a figure that many still detest.
Yet, whatever one's views, one has to concede
That her teenage years were uneasy indeed.
No sooner was the wretched child crowned French Queen
Than she found herself a widow – at eighteen.
Her boy-husband, King Francis the Second, died;
But, far worse, his witch of a mother survived.
Catherine de Médicis was an old foe
Of the late Mary of Guise who, as we know,
Was the new widow's mother. Mothers-in-law!
Catherine (politely) showed Mary the door.

The poor girl, for the first time in thirteen years,
Was sent back to Scotland. She shed bitter tears.
The luxury of the French court she exchanged
For the cold north. Scotland, remember, had changed:
No longer Catholic, the Reformation,
Under good John Knox, had transformed the nation.

Lethington and the Protestants feared the worst,
Yet Mary made no attempt (at least at first)
To turn back the clock. Lethington stayed in post
And (the move that astounded them all the most)
She allowed herself to be lectured by Knox.
The Scottish Catholics, bless their cotton socks,

The Tudors

Were somewhat bemused. What was less widely known
Was that Mary coveted the English throne.
Her strategy was startlingly clever –
Upset the Protestants and she would never,
Ever, stand a chance of asserting her claim
To Elizabeth's place. A dangerous game,
Perhaps, but Mary's natural condition
Was ruthless (if covert) driving ambition.

Three years after her return, all fell apart.
Despite the Queen's encouraging early start,
She married badly in 1564.
Lord Darnley was her half-first cousin, therefore
A Tudor too. He'd been born on English soil
(Unlike Mary), so was somehow more 'royal'.
The marriage made Elizabeth's blood boil,
As you can well imagine. Jealousy, too,
May have played its part for, between me and you,
Darnley was tall, good-looking and quite a catch.

It proved, however, a deplorable match.
Henry Stuart, Earl of Darnley, was vicious,
Arrogant, wayward, moody and capricious.
Mary's Protestant ministers disapproved.
Their leader, the Earl of Murray, was removed
And fled abroad. The writing was on the wall:
Mary never favoured Protestants at all.
Promoting once again the Catholic creed,
The Queen appointed in her hour of need
An Italian as her Chief Minister,
One David Rizzio. Nothing sinister
Need be read into their 'personal' greetings,
Or their over-long, 'private' midnight meetings.
Rizzio was meticulous and zealous –
Darnley, in turn, ridiculously jealous.

He stormed into Mary's closet late one night
With a gang of nobles, spoiling for a fight.

Rhyming History

He butchered Rizzio before her very eyes.
Mary was six months' pregnant, and it's some surprise
She didn't miscarry. In June '66
She gave birth to a wee boy, James. Catholics
Rejoiced. Elizabeth didn't. Mary's heir
Revived the whole wretched succession affair –
Which is why Parliament became so keen
To wring an answer from their reluctant Queen.

Mary, Queen of Scots, meanwhile, plotted revenge
On her vile, murderous husband. To avenge
Rizzio became her preoccupation.

Watched by a tremulous and wary nation,
Mary conspired (allegedly) with one Bothwell
To kill the beast. Did she manage it? Who can tell?
What is certain is that Darnley breathed his last
In an explosion, victim of a huge blast

The Tudors

In a house at Kirk o'Field. He'd been strangled.
His body was discovered charred and mangled.

Bothwell blew the place up, no doubt about that,
And bumped Darnley off to boot, the dirty rat.
Mary had urged her dearly beloved spouse,
Just days before, to go there. She found the house.
She chose the spot. She left the poor loser there.
Alone. And vulnerable. And unaware.

Make of that what you will. Bothwell was half-mad –
Depraved, degenerate and thoroughly bad.
Yet Mary married the wretch. The prime suspect!
Her subjects rebelled. What else did she expect?
Within a few short months, the Queen was deposed.
Baby James, sooner than he might have supposed,
Inherited the throne. Bothwell fled abroad.   **1567**
Murray was recalled as Regent, his reward

Rhyming History

For loyalty and good sense. The wayward Queen
Was banished to Loch Leven. Picture the scene:
Abandoned by her people, denied her throne,
Her character in tatters, deprived, alone.

All very well, you may say, but so what?
What's this to do with England? Quite a lot.
Mary escaped in 1568,   **1568**
But failed to recover her crown. Her fate
Was determined in the main, from that date,
By her cousin Elizabeth. For years
She was England's prisoner. It appears
That neither France nor Spain, though Catholic,
When the chips were down, cared a fiddlestick
For this unruly, irreligious Queen.
Elizabeth, for her part, wasn't keen.
She could hardly lend Mary her support
Against Murray, a Protestant – her 'sort'.
Conversely, cousin Mary was a royal:
Elizabeth's instincts were deeply loyal.

Some dilemma. She was in no hurry
To decide. So, she invited Murray
To put the case against the Scottish Queen.
Mary herself, as might have been foreseen,
Kept her counsel. The evidence was slight:
So-called 'casket letters' were brought to light,
Which half-hinted at her implication
In the dastardly assassination
Of her husband Darnley. This was not proved.
Neither, however, was the case disproved.
The final verdict was inconclusive.

Mary was livid, some say abusive –
In private, at least. But her fate was sealed.
She had come to England. She had appealed
To her cousin. She'd neither won nor lost,
But for nineteen years she counted the cost.
At liberty she posed the gravest threat,
The 'Catholic alternative', and yet
Elizabeth refused to contemplate
Her death. The security of the state
Was in some jeopardy. Plot after plot
Was hatched in Mary's name. Like it or not,
The Queen of Scots finally lost her head,
And most agreed she was better off dead.

Nautical adventures

We're running ahead of ourselves. Let's go back.
We need to set off on a different tack:
The sea. Hawkins and Drake now take centre-stage –
Sea-faring heroes of a new golden age.
Commerce was the spur. A healthy trade in wool
Had, for decades, kept the nation's coffers full.
Men felt little need to look further afield
Than Flanders. Sheep had kept them pretty well-heeled.
Then came the depression. Catastrophe loomed.
The markets collapsed. The wool trade was doomed.

Rhyming History

For some years past, the Spanish and Portuguese
Had amassed huge wealth from foreign colonies:
Portugal in coastal Africa, Brazil,
And the East Indies; with Spain, for good or ill,
Occupying most of South America –
Chile and Peru and, north of Panama,
The Caribbean Islands and Mexico.
The Spanish Empire, even as Empires go,
Was vastly rich. I have no hesitation
In roundly condemning the exploitation:
The Spanish (and Portuguese) were not traders,
But sea-bandits, asset-strippers, mere raiders.

Spain's treasure chests were full to overflowing
With gold bullion, and there was no knowing
What undiscovered riches yet lay in store.

The English looked on with envy. Furthermore,
Pope Alexander, in 1494,
Had drawn an imaginary dotted line –
Can you think of anything more asinine? –
South from the Azores. All new discoveries
To the west belonged to Spain and, if you please,
The rest to Portugal! This, without a doubt,
Was carefully contrived to keep England out.

Well, that's something of an exaggeration.
Henry the Seventh's main preoccupation
Was sound finance, domestic stability
And peace. Men of nautical ability,
Like Columbus, who applied to him for aid
Were turned down flat. Once the division was made –
By the Pope, of the globe into east and west –
The English were effectively dispossessed:
An irrelevant and excluded nation.
The wool crisis worsened the situation.
England had to explore new routes overseas
Or die. Despite protests from the Portuguese,

The Tudors

Sea-adventurers started to ply their trade
Down the west African coast. Fortunes were made,
By men like John Lok, in ivory and gold.

But the main source of excitement, so we're told,
Were the Spice Islands in the far distant east.
Interest in oriental routes increased
With the informed speculation of John Dee –
An expert in the arts of astrology,
Mathematics and marine geography –
That there existed a path, north-east, by sea,
By which Asia could be reached with ease. Ice-free,
This passage (once found!) was the obvious way
To sail to the Spice Islands. On a good day,
The learned Doctor Dee was second to none,
But he was well capable, like anyone,
Of the odd 'inexactitude'. This was one such.

Rhyming History

Not, however, that it mattered very much.
An expedition in 1553,
Led by Sir Hugh Willoughby and backed by Dee,
Failed in its mission. Sir Hugh was lost at sea.
His junior, Richard Chancellor, sailed on –
He had no other option, Willoughby gone.

He continued north round the coast of Norway
And into the White Sea. There he had to stay,
For land, he discovered, was blocking his way.
Chancellor disembarked. The next thing we know,
Trade talks had started with the Tsar of Moscow –
Not too bad an outcome, as disasters go!

The English Muscovy Company survived
For centuries, and trade with Russia thrived.

The north-east passage, though, proved an illusion.
Ditto the north-west: this too caused confusion.
Just as Dee, as we've seen, had dreamt of a route
North-east to China, so others followed suit –
Entirely in the opposite direction.
I have no particular expectation
That this will be of the slightest interest,
But efforts to reach China by the north-west
Also failed. Several seamen did their best:
Frobisher, Davis, both enterprising chaps,
Underrated by posterity, perhaps.

So, back to the Caribbean. Spain forbade
All trading with her colonies. This was bad.
The odd licence would be granted, though rarely.
Her monopoly was granted unfairly,
As we've noted, by the Pope. It's no surprise
That England, with her keen eye for enterprise,
Envied the Spanish their unearned, easy wealth.
She wanted, quite simply, some of it herself.

The Tudors

John Hawkins

The first great sea-warrior was John Hawkins.
His philosophy of life was, 'Who dares, wins'.
This fine sailor, commander and diplomat
Determined, absolutely off his own bat,
To break the Spanish monopoly in trade.
Bully for him. Now prepare to be dismayed:
His traffic was in slaves. Some reports I've read
Exonerate Hawkins, claim he was well-bred,
Humane, and a general all-round 'good guy' –
A 'man of his time'. I think I'd rather die
Than subscribe to this glib justification
For such a vicious form of exploitation.

There's no avoiding John Hawkins, however.
By the standards of the time he was clever,
Far-sighted and shrewd. The west African coast
Was where he purchased his slaves. What riles me most
Is that some say he had great charm. Some excuse
For callous, inhuman and brutal abuse.

Be that as it may, there was massive demand
For slaves in the West Indies. They could command
High prices. Hawkins' first trip was a 'success'.
For his second, Queen Elizabeth, no less,
Provided capital – including a ship.
This did much to poison the relationship,
Already in a delicate state, with Spain.
This time Hawkins headed for the Spanish main –
A bolder, more profitable exercise.
Our friend Philip the Second (surprise, surprise)
Objected. He was livid. He felt ill-used.
Spain's monopoly had been roundly abused –
By an Englishman! The King was not amused.

By the time Hawkins set sail for the third time,   **1567-69**
The Spanish were ready. Hawkins, in his prime,

91

Rhyming History

Was getting cocky. Trading in slaves was slow.
Spanish intransigence kept his income low.
Worse still, his ships were hit by a hurricane
And battered. To limp home would have been insane,
So he put in for repair near Veracruz,
At San Juan de Ulua. The bad news?
This was a Spanish harbour! The fleet from Spain
Was expected daily. What was there to gain,
Men asked, from staying at anchor? Hawkins' force
Was weak and vulnerable. He had recourse,
Therefore, to strategy. His real position
Was stronger than his ships' fragile condition:
His fleet was anchored in a strategic spot
Outside the harbour, past which, like it or not,
All the Spanish treasure vessels had to sail.
Hawkins held the advantage. He couldn't fail.

He offered safe passage to the Spanish fleet,
In exchange for their guarantee (this was neat)
Of safety for his ships. The compact was made.
John Hawkins kept his word. He was unafraid.
Also naïve. He'd no sooner turned his back
Than the Spanish launched a treacherous attack.
Two-thirds of the English fleet (four ships) were lost.
Hawkins discovered too late, and to his cost,
The price of keeping faith. His junior, Drake,
Survived. It would have been a costly mistake
Had he not! Their homeward voyages were grim,
Hawkins' in particular. No one blamed him,
But only a handful of his gallant crew
Made it back to dry land – the fortunate few.

The knives were now out. This was a turning point.
Anglo-Spanish relations were out of joint –
Badly. The hawks called for war. They always do.
But England was weak. This Elizabeth knew.
Any war would be fought out on the high seas:
The country could quickly be brought to her knees.

The Tudors

Still a mere decade into the good Queen's reign,
With finances under the usual strain,
Defences were in a state of disrepair.

It was Elizabeth's own private nightmare
That Philip would invade. Cecil, to be fair,
Shared her forebodings. He'd long been in despair
At the state of the fleet. When Hawkins retired
From active seamanship, still widely admired
(Despite his fateful voyage), he, Cecil knew,
Was the man for the job. What did Hawkins do?
He embarked upon root-and-branch reconstruction
Of the navy, spearheading the introduction
Of new financial systems. He fought corruption,
Replaced leading personnel, declared war on waste.
His radical ways weren't to everyone's taste,
Nor was the great sea-change accomplished overnight.

But as Cecil's adviser, then (in his own right)
As Naval Treasurer, no man laboured harder
Than Hawkins to plan for the Spanish Armada.

Rhyming History

Sir Francis Drake

The greatest seaman of the age was Drake.
Eight years Hawkins' junior (give or take),
Francis hailed from Devon, of humble birth.
His father was a farmer, down-to-earth,
Hardworking, and a preacher too, we're told –
A Protestant. When Drake was nine years old,
An outbreak of Catholic discontent
Caused the whole family to flee – to Kent.
They were forced to live in an old, damp hulk
On the Thames estuary. Rather than sulk –
Not in his nature – Drake took to the sea.
As a teenager, eager as could be,
Young Francis (who had his living to earn)
Learned more about ships than there was to learn.
Conditions were tough. He sailed to and fro
Between North Sea ports. As apprenticeships go,
It was perfect. When his old captain died,
He left Drake his ship: he was that satisfied.

Drake enlisted with Hawkins. Ever keen,
And able, he caught the eye of the Queen.
Privateering it was that won him fame:
'Ambition' might have been his middle name.
Relations with Spain were at a new low:
The Queen encouraged him to 'have a go' –
Covertly, though. Cecil would get upset,
But Elizabeth was pro-Drake – you bet!
In 1572 he set sail,   **1572**
Bound for the Caribbean. Tooth and nail
He fought, terrorizing the Spanish main.
He hijacked a fantastic treasure train
To the value of forty thousand pounds.
Drake's devilry and daring knew no bounds.

He returned in 1573   **1573**
To discover that, temporarily,

The Tudors

Peace terms were on the agenda with Spain.
To have set off a-plundering again
Would have been a touch 'undiplomatic'.
So, for some years, Drake's career was static –
In nautical terms, at least. Reports state
That he served in Ireland, though from what date
It's difficult precisely to discern.

Events were soon to take a global turn.
In 1577 we learn   **1577**
Of an ambitious new sea enterprise
In the planning. It comes as no surprise
That they called for Drake. John Dee was intent
On discovering his new continent –
Terra Australis. Others were hell-bent
On whipping the Spanish. The government
Sought new trade outlets. What tempted them most
Was South America's Pacific coast.
Elizabeth herself gave strong backing
To this great adventure. Only lacking
Was a leader. She in person chose Drake –
A stroke of genius and no mistake.
The Queen spoke her mind. She was deeply aggrieved
At "divers injuries" that she had received
And "would gladly be revenged on the King of Spain".
No doubt about it at all, her meaning was plain.
Drake set sail, as it were, by royal commission –
With Elizabeth's full blessing and permission.

Of the crew that set out, two hundred men,
Fewer than sixty returned: three in ten.
Of the five ships, just one – the *Golden Hind,*
Drake's own – made it home. Four were left behind.
But that's a false picture. Never before
In England's history, in peace or war,
Had one voyage so inspired the nation
As Drake's famous circumnavigation.

Rhyming History

He reached Brazil in spring '78.**1578**
There his scheming deputy met his fate –
One Thomas Doughty. An old friend of Drake's,
He turned mutineer (we all make mistakes).
With ambitions well above his station,
Thomas was hanged for insubordination
And inciting revolt. Back in control,
Captain Drake pressed on south, now on a roll.
Along the line he pruned his modest fleet
By two: his storage ships were obsolete –
Surplus to requirements. Seven months on,
Half his ships' victuals were already gone.

In late August 1578
Drake's fleet sailed into the Magellan Strait –
And it took just sixteen days to pass through.
Instead of relishing the perfect view –
The Pacific Ocean an azure blue,
Uncharted waters, exciting and new,
All that Drake had been looking forward to –
He ran into a hurricane-force gale,
A tempest on a truly epic scale.

Only the *Golden Hind* weathered the storm.
Driven back, almost as far as Cape Horn,
Drake rallied, sailing up the western coast
Past Chile and Peru. What pleased him most
Was the ease with which he met with success.

He caused the Spanish maximum distress:
They simply weren't prepared for Drake's onslaught.
He attacked all targets, and where he fought,
He won. By spring 1579**1579**
His ship was well below its waterline,
Heavy with Spanish coin, silver and gold,
With precious pearls and gemstones – wealth untold.

The Tudors

Finally, he remembered Doctor Dee.
Pushing north, to the forty-eighth degree,
He sought the north-west passage. Drake, we're told,
Was never one who much enjoyed the cold.
Here it was freezing! He didn't stay long.

Firmly convinced that Dee had got it wrong,
He planned to strike out across the ocean,
But not before fostering the notion
Of claiming 'New Albion' for the Queen –
That's California. There'd never been
Such a loyal subject as Francis Drake.

Undertaken for his sovereign's sake,
His trail-blazing circumnavigation
Caused widespread patriotic jubilation.

On ploughed Drake in summer '79,
West across the Pacific. All was fine:

Rhyming History

Weather, discipline, the following winds.
After two months he reached the Philippines,
Then the Moluccas, where he bought spices –
Top-quality cloves, at knock-down prices.
Sailing from the Spice Islands (as they're called),
His ship foundered on a reef. Drake, appalled,
Jettisoned cloves (and guns) to offload weight.

Never a man to 'hum' or hesitate,
Drake's precipitate action saved the day.
His flagship slipped off the rock… and away –
Thanks partly to him, and to the high tide.
Management or miracle? You decide.

The rest seemed simple by comparison.
Drake rounded the Cape of Good Hope, then on,
Up the African coast, past the Azores
And back to Plymouth. He'd settled old scores,
Avenged the good Queen, cocked a snook at Rome,
Terrorized Spain – and now was safely home.   **1580**

Three years he'd been away. "Does the Queen live?"
Was his famous question. Would she forgive,
He wondered, his piratical actions?
Which of her Council's two rival factions
Was in the ascendant? Who in, who out?

His destiny rested, he had no doubt,
On the present state of relations with Spain.
His conduct had given them cause to complain,
And complain they had! Elizabeth, though,
Cared not a fig for that. All Europe should know
Where her loyalties lay. On board the *Golden Hind*,
The valiant Queen eloquently spoke her mind:

By conferring a knighthood upon Francis Drake,
She nailed her colours to the mast, for England's sake.

The Tudors

Spain and the Netherlands

Foreign affairs had been in a turbulent state
Ever since we left them – in 1568.
Philip of Spain still coveted the English throne,
But preferred to see Elizabeth overthrown
By her own subjects than by foreign invasion.
Mary Stuart's flight to England would occasion,
So the Spanish King hoped, widespread civil unrest –
A potent new focus for Catholic protest.
But Philip was cautious and, though he did his best
To fuel the flames, he eschewed direct action.
Trouble in the Netherlands was the distraction,
Where a strong anti-Catholic rebel faction
Undermined Spanish rule more than some realise.
England was lucky, and it comes as no surprise
To find Elizabeth seeking, off her own bat,
To support the insurgents. It was tit for tat:

While Spain wanted England back in Catholic hands,
The Queen backed the Protestants in the Netherlands.

Catholic unrest

What was the net effect of Mary's arrival?
Some feared for Elizabeth's very survival.
There were indeed a number of plots. One de Spes,
The Spanish Ambassador, sought various ways
Of fomenting mischief and, wherever he went,
Stirred up the waters of Catholic discontent.
With Roberto di Ridolfi, a Florentine,
He hatched a plot, early in 1569,
To free Mary, sack Cecil, and depose the Queen.

The Catholic Duke of Norfolk, a mere has-been,
Joined these reprobate foreigners. His chief reason
Was personal hatred of Cecil. His treason
Lay in his scheme to restore the Catholic Church
In the person of 'Queen' Mary. Left in the lurch
By Alva, Philip's ruthless representative
In the Netherlands, the plot failed. Lucky to live,
Norfolk fled. He hadn't finished yet though, the fool.
Failing to topple a Queen, you'd think (as a rule)
It might be sensible to call it a day.
But Norfolk was fickle. That wasn't his way.
In secret league with powerful Lords in the north –
Earls of Northumberland, Westmoreland and so forth –
A great rebellion had already been planned
To restore Catholicism throughout the land.

Elizabeth's spies, however, were on the case:
Norfolk was apprehended and in deep disgrace.
Without him, the northern revolt went on apace.
Remember the earlier Pilgrimage of Grace,
In good King Henry's time? Successfully suppressed,
Its legacy lingered on, it must be confessed,

With a myriad of old scores to be settled.
The Queen, unimpressed and not a little nettled,
Yet ever cautious where Catholics were concerned,
Unleashed her vengeance.
                    Whole swathes of land were burned,
Hundreds executed, and some hard lessons learned.

A brief respite. The overall situation
Was not helped by the Queen's excommunication.
Pope Pius the Fifth declared, quite out of the blue,
Elizabeth excommunicate. Very few,
Truth to tell, took much notice and, in retrospect,
The Bull was a damp squib. What did Pius expect?
For a start, he failed to consult Philip of Spain
Before publishing his decree. This was insane.
The Pope called on his subjects, pious and devout,
To 'remove' the Queen. But who could carry this out?
Only Philip, and he was livid with the Pope
For his lack of courtesy and tact. What a dope!
I say 'only Philip', but that's not strictly true.
Catholics at home were uncertain what to do:
Stay loyal to Rome, or to their Protestant Queen?
An awkward dilemma, if you see what I mean.

But the Bull was poorly phrased, its language too loose,
And many a Catholic made this the excuse
For ignoring it. The Pope, for instance, had said
That the Queen had taken the title 'Supreme Head',
Whereas Elizabeth insisted, all along,
On 'Supreme Governor'. The Bull was just plain wrong.

The Ridolfi plot

Quite apart from conflicts of interest at home,
The sudden interference of the Pope in Rome
Gave succour to England's foes. A second vile plot –
Led by Ridolfi again, believe it or not –

Was laid in '71 against the Queen's life.
Thomas Norfolk would take Mary Stuart to wife,
With Mary crowned Queen in place of Elizabeth.
For his treachery, Norfolk was sentenced to death,
And not before time. Elizabeth resisted,
But in the Commons the Puritans insisted.
They also argued for Mary's execution,
Which indeed appeared a natural solution
To the danger posed by the naughty Scottish Queen.
It is idle to speculate what might have been,
Had she perished for her sins. Be that as it may,
Mary was spared. She lived to fight another day.
Norfolk had his head chopped off. Good riddance, I say.

Nobody knows for sure what part Mary did play
In the Ridolfi Plot (as it came to be known),
But its sole purpose was to place her on the throne.
The Pope was almost certainly implicated,
As were Philip and de Spes, who contemplated,
After Mary's accession, the kind of influence
Not seen since Mary Tudor's day. To them it made sense.

It was Cecil's secret service that stopped the rot.
By torture and surveillance, they exposed the plot.
But the threat to the Queen lived on, like it or not,
In Elizabeth's cousin, the slippery Scot.

Di Ridolfi himself (in his wisdom) ensured,
When the plot was unearthed, he was safely abroad.
He served in the Florentine Senate, we're told,
And died in his bed. He was eighty years old.

A proposal

Further grave events in 1572
May explain why Protestant anxieties grew.
Spain had taxed Elizabeth beyond endurance,
So England acceded (a kind of insurance)

The Tudors

To the Treaty of Blois – an alliance with France.
This followed another matrimonial dance,
In which Elizabeth and the Duke of Anjou
Jumped through the usual hoops, pretending to woo.
The third son of 'Queen' Catherine de Médicis,
Anjou hadn't a chance. All but the blind could see –
And see they did – that this was a hopeless mismatch.
Good Queen Bess, pushing forty, was hardly a catch,
But far more telling than the obstacle of age
Was religion. Imagine the Protestant rage
Had Elizabeth got hitched to a Catholic!
Bigotry. Prejudice. Don't they just make you sick?
Be that as it may, the wedding plans fizzled out.
But the Treaty of Blois stood, seen (I have no doubt)
As a shield against future Spanish aggression.

Religious tensions abroad

Two new crises followed in rapid succession.
Rebellious Protestants in the Netherlands
Sought to throw off the Spanish yoke. Marauding bands
Succeeded in four provinces out of thirteen.
This may have been welcomed by our Protestant Queen,
But she had to show caution. Her instincts, of course,
Favoured William of Orange. Yet to use force,
On his side, against the Spanish, would have been mad.

She knew there was little benefit to be had
In alienating Philip without good cause,
But the French dimension gave occasion to pause:
William could turn to France without her support –
An unholy alliance. The Queen was thus caught
Between the proverbial rock and a hard place.
Yet she managed, the wily old bird, to save face:
She backed the Dutch Protestants wherever she could,
Covertly and with minimum risk. She was good,
It has to be said, at the art of double-bluff –
And, with English interests at heart, fair enough.

Rhyming History

There followed sixteen years of plotting and intrigue,
The details of which are well out of my league.

St. Bartholomew's Day

The next dreadful event in this seminal year
Was a massacre. Be ready to shed a tear.

French society was for centuries riven
With civil strife born of religious division.
Protestant folk in France were known as Huguenots,
But the land as a whole, as everyone knows,
Was overwhelmingly Catholic. However,
One Admiral de Coligny – astute, clever,
And a leading Huguenot – persuaded the King,
Charles the Ninth (Catholic), to stake everything
On waging war, in the Netherlands, against Spain.
Exactly what either man thought France stood to gain
From such a wilful and frankly hare-brained campaign
Beggars belief, and still remains a mystery.

The French were torn to shreds. The rest is history.
Catherine de Médicis, Charles' aged mother –
Our friend the Duke of Anjou was his kid brother –
Strongly resented the Admiral's influence:
A Huguenot, he had to go – just common sense.
But the plot to 'remove' Coligny was derailed
When a bungled assassination attempt failed.
Catherine, allied to the rival House of Guise,
Was startled when she learned that son Charles,
                                   if you please,
Proposed an inquiry into the 'accident'.
Too well aware of what exposure would have meant,
Catherine urged her weak and vacillating son
To rid France of all Huguenots – every one!
"D'accord, Maman," dit-il. No sooner said, than done.

The Tudors

On the morning of the feast of St. Bartholomew
(That's August the 24th) 1572,
Charles gave his personal order for the 'purgation'
Of Parisian Huguenots (not the whole nation).

Only those of noble birth were at first specified,
But the mad mob, once roused, proceeded to override
The King's commands. 3,000 Huguenots were slain
In Paris alone. The following day, in vain,
The King ordered a halt to the slaughter. It spread.
In total, some 50,000 victims lay dead –
In places as far-flung as Lyon, Bourges, Bordeaux,
Rouen and Orléans. Many a Huguenot
Was spared, God be thanked, but Protestants far and wide,
Elizabeth included, were left horrified.

Rhyming History

The wayward Pope put Elizabeth in a spin,
By announcing that he would hold it "no great sin"
To "send the Queen out of this world". Under pressure
From the Puritans, the Commons passed a measure
Raising fines for recusancy to twenty pounds
(A massive sum), affording Elizabeth grounds
For fearing a Catholic backlash. The same Act   **1581**
Made it treason to convert to Rome – and that's a fact.

A new wave of Jesuit missionaries
Were tried for adherence to "the Queen's enemies".
This expression, of course, in a word, meant the Pope.
Gregory had queered their pitch. They hadn't a hope.
Edmund Campion was one such executed
For preaching the faith. The charge was convoluted,
But basically treason. Gregory raised the stakes.
Elizabeth, for her own and for her subjects' sakes,
Was ready to consent to harsher penalties
Against these wretched Jesuits from overseas.
Some brave martyrs suffered death (the ultimate price),
As many a priest made the final sacrifice.

However, lest we all get too pessimistic,
Pray attend to one remarkable statistic:
Fewer than two hundred and fifty men in all –
No greater number can historians recall –
Died for their Catholic faith in Elizabeth's reign.
For those of you hard of hearing, I'll say it again:
Just two hundred and fifty priests at the very most,
While in Spain and the Netherlands, Protestants were toast!
Elizabeth's wisdom was greatly to her credit.
Her sense and forbearance saved England. There, I've said it.

As matters went from bad to worse, she kept her cool.
Extreme deeds require urgent measures, as a rule –
But the Queen far preferred diplomacy and tact,
And kept her powder dry till it was time to act.

France, Spain and the Netherlands

The Netherlands remained a dreadful trouble spot
And Elizabeth, whether she liked it or not,
Couldn't opt out as a mere observer for long.
William of Orange, as she'd known all along,
Would turn to the French if she withheld her support.
The Dutch Prince was becoming increasingly fraught:
He was cornered, vulnerable, isolated,
And stony-broke. The Queen even contemplated –
This no word of a joke – declaring war on Spain,
But quickly drew back from the brink and thought again.
Indeed, she opened up fresh negotiations,
With Philip, to establish better relations –
A decision at once politic and clever.

The irksome Spanish Ambassador, however,
A certain de Mendoza (a new appointment)
Proved a most unfortunate fly in the ointment.
He worked hard to undermine the Queen's position,
At home and abroad. Prince William's condition
Was desperate. He turned to Catherine's fourth son,
The volatile, capricious Duke of Alençon,
To lend his weight and backing to the Dutch revolt.

The Duke failed. It was hardly Elizabeth's fault,
As some argued, that Spain continued to hold sway.
Alençon tried to drag her into the affray
By wooing the tough old bird (now aged forty-five),
Which at least kept Lord Burghley's fragile hopes alive
Of an heir, albeit fathered by a French Duke.

Elizabeth played up, earning the brisk rebuke
Of the Puritan contingent. Frisky, no less,
She displayed a distinct lack of taste in her dress,
Manners and demeanour. She overreached herself:
One final fling before being left on the shelf.

The Queen fawned on Alençon like a little dog;
She called the Duke (he was French, after all), her 'frog'.

Their unedifying courtship lasted three years,
On and off, before ending (like the rest) in tears.
However serious she'd been, the net effect
On the 'war' was limited. Spain was still dead set
On keeping her Dutch dominions, but the Queen
(Sagacious as ever) was loth to intervene.
Her support for Alençon, at best half-hearted,
Was at worst a sham. When the two 'lovers' parted,
In 1580, little had been accomplished.
Elizabeth won time (perhaps that's all she'd wished),
While Alençon was forced to face the real drama –
A showdown with Philip's top general, Parma.
In 1582 Alençon's Dutch campaign   **1582**
Collapsed. Elizabeth never saw him again.

When he died (two years later) the Queen was distressed,
Kept to her room for days, though it must be confessed

110

That throughout their courtship she had kept a cool head,
Politically, at least. With Alençon dead,
Elizabeth's little *amours* came to an end.
Her favourites drove her ministers round the bend,
And would continue to do so – men like Leicester,
And Essex, though the latter would sorely test her.

But her love life was done. The succession question
Took on a new aspect. The very suggestion
Of Mary, Queen of Scots, inheriting the throne
Was anathema still. England's fate was unknown.

The Throckmorton plot

In 1583 the most deadly plot yet   **1583**
Was hatched against Elizabeth. This dire new threat,
Real and immediate, against the Queen's life
Came from France, Spain and Rome.
                                    Rumours had long been rife
Of a foul alliance between Philip, the Pope,
And Henri, duc de Guise, in France. Only the scope,
Detail and timing of their design were unknown.
But moves were afoot to put Mary on the throne,
That much was certain. The Secretary of State,
Francis Walsingham, suspected, at any rate,
That an attack was imminent from overseas.

His undercover agents in the House of Guise
Assured him of it. Walsingham's network of spies
Was active at home and abroad. It's no surprise,
Therefore, that the English link was finally found:
A certain Francis Throckmorton was run to ground.
A staunch Roman Catholic and widely travelled,
He was tortured, and the plot quickly unravelled.

Walsingham suspected he'd been a go-between –
The intermediary for the Scottish Queen

And the odious Mendoza. This wasn't proved,
But Philip's Ambassador was swiftly removed,
Spitting fury as he went. Throckmorton confessed
And begged for mercy. Walsingham wasn't impressed:
The traitor went to the block. Mary had connived   **1584**
(Or had she?) at the conspiracy. Yet she survived.

Sir Francis Walsingham

Francis Walsingham, spymaster *par excellence,*
First came to notice as Ambassador to France
Between 1570 and '73.
Although spy catching was his speciality,
He handled some very tricky situations
Regarding the marriage negotiations
Between Elizabeth and the Duke of Anjou –
And, some years later, with his younger brother too,
The Duke of Alençon (far from simple matters,
Given that both fellows were as mad as hatters).
He made a strong impression on the Queen's behalf
And soon became a valued member of her staff.

Elizabeth, of course, chose neither of the Dukes,
Which earned for Walsingham the mildest of rebukes.
His negotiations failed. That suited her fine –
She'd managed to attain the age of forty-nine
Without a husband. Walsingham had done his best,
But fallen short. In the Queen's eyes, he passed the test!

After the massacre of St. Bartholomew,
Walsingham kept his cool, one of the very few.
The intervention of France in the Netherlands
Was Cecil's worst fear. Francis, a safe pair of hands,
Successfully managed to hold Spain at arm's length,
Whilst keeping the French on side – a feat of some strength.
The Treaty of Blois was his. He concluded it.
In diplomatic affairs, Walsingham was fit.

The Tudors

The assassination of William of Orange

Elizabeth did her utmost to avoid war,
But the major event of 1584
Brought it ever nearer. She (and the whole nation)
Were dismayed to learn of the assassination
Of William of Orange ('the Silent', so-called).
The Queen was horrified. Protestants were appalled:
Their prospects of survival in the Netherlands
Were never worse. Antwerp fell into Spanish hands.
Moreover, the troublesome Guise faction in France
Was leading poor Henry the Third a merry dance,
Threatening a Catholic alliance with Spain.
The dread implications of this were all too plain.

Elizabeth, at last, was forced to recognise
The risk to her own person. This opened her eyes.
For the very first time, in August '85,   **1585**
In a bid to keep the Protestant cause alive,
England intervened directly in Dutch affairs.
In a move that caught the great Parma unawares,
The Earl of Leicester was despatched with a large force
Of 7,000 well-armed men. Leicester, of course,
Had long been a special favourite of the Queen.
As Sir Robert Dudley (this we've already seen),
He was a serious suitor. Handsome, witty,
And Protestant, some considered it a pity
That his suit failed. There were others, though, suspicious
Of Leicester's ambition. He could be capricious,
Arrogant, far too inclined to quarrel, and vain –
Though this made him, some said, the perfect foil for Spain.
Be that as it may, he headed the Queen's mission
To the Netherlands where, without her permission,
He was appointed Governor. She was livid.
She'd expressly told Robert, whatever he did,
Not to give the impression that she, England's Queen,
Was sovereign over the Dutch. Leicester came clean,

Apologised (grovelled, even), so no harm done.
But he persevered in acting like Number One:
He quarrelled with his officers, spent far too much,
And somehow even managed to upset the Dutch.

Leicester achieved little. Far from winning the war,
He left the Dutch Protestants worse off than before.
He returned home at the tail end of '86,   **1586**
The Queen vexed, and the Netherlands still in a fix.

William of Orange's assassination
Stiffened England's resolute determination
To protect Elizabeth. Across the nation,
Men subscribed to a Bond of Association
Whereby, were the Sovereign assassinated,
Those persons "by whom the deed was perpetrated" –
Or "for whom" – would be "prosecuted to the death".
Note the "for whom": the murder of Elizabeth
Might well occur with Mary Stuart's approval,
Though absent of proof. Good Queen Bess's 'removal'
Need only be seen to benefit the Scots' Queen
For her to die. What, however, was unforeseen –
By the subscribers to the Bond, at least – was this:
"For whom" would run counter to natural justice.

Elizabeth spotted this herself. Mary's son,
Young James (a potential successor), was just one
"For whom", it could be argued, the fell deed was done,
Yet no one was suggesting… The ills of the clause
Outweighed the benefits. There was a well-timed pause.
When, in 1585, a Statute was passed
Enacting the Bond, the "for whom" phrase was recast:
Foreknowledge of a plot or a conspiracy
Was required, with mere advantage no guarantee
Of guilt. Had not the Bond been altered in this way,
James might never have been King. I'm happy to say,
It was Elizabeth's foresight that saved the day.

The Tudors

Mary, Queen of Scots

Mary Stuart's sad life was drawing to a close.
In 1586 (quite how, nobody knows)
Francis Walsingham unearthed the Babington Plot.
Whether he 'set it up', as some claim, I know not,
But Mary was led to believe, somehow at least,
That with the help of God, and the odd friendly priest,
She could safely correspond with plotters abroad –
In France. This was a folly she could ill afford.
Walsingham intercepted her correspondence –
Read her every rash, unguarded utterance.

This plot, like the rest, would place Mary on the throne,
With Elizabeth put to death, or overthrown.
Babington, one of the Queen of Scots' ex-pages,
Sought Mary's approval. For what seemed like ages,
No answer was forthcoming. Then at last it came:
The Scots' Queen gave her consent. It was not just game,
But set and match to Walsingham. Mary was tried
And found guilty, the verdict welcomed countrywide.

Parliament, People, Council – all were as one:
The wicked Scottish Queen should die for what she'd done.
Enough was enough. Elizabeth was at risk.
Let the punishment be death, and let it be brisk.

The stumbling block was Queen Elizabeth the First,
Mary's cousin in blood. She had neither the thirst,
Nor appetite, for a royal execution,
So settled upon a compromise solution:
After three months' delay and prevarication
She signed the death warrant, but caused consternation
By neglecting to despatch it! Leicester and Co –
Lord Burghley, Walsingham, and others in the know –
Finally, and without Elizabeth's consent,
Sent it off themselves, and we all know what that meant.

February the 8th, 1587,   **1587**
Was the day that Mary's soul took flight for Heaven.
The scene was Fotheringhay Castle, the Great Hall.

She mounted the scaffold, hardly shaking at all,
And laid her head upon the block. With dignity,
Courage, and a tragic pride (a pity to see),
She went to her death a martyr. Catholics wept.
Protestants rejoiced. Elizabeth barely slept,
Though whether from the bells of London ringing out
Or from her own dreadful guilt, there's some room for doubt.
Livid with her Council, the Queen ranted and raved,
Unaware that her own precious self had been saved.
She'd never seen Mary as a figure of hate,
But rather (her own phrase) "the daughter of debate".

The Tudors

The Scots were incensed. Mary's twenty-year-old son,
James, put on a show of anger, but fooled no one.
He had never much subscribed to his mother's cause –
He barely knew her – and, after a decent pause,
Kept his head down. His chances of the succession
Had been much enhanced by his mother's 'transgression'.

War with Spain

The stage, though, was finally set for war with Spain.
Philip had little now to lose and all to gain,
Or so he thought. With the Scots' Queen out of the way,
The English throne was his for the taking. Some say –
And I offer no view – that he welcomed her death.

Be that as it may, when Mary drew her last breath,
War was inevitable. Philip scorned James' right,
Dubbed him a heretic. In his own name he'd fight
Or, as he pretended, in the Catholic cause.
Spain was all-powerful. France, plagued by civil wars,
Was an irrelevance. Spanish troops were the best,
The finest in Europe – equipped for any test.

England's strength, however, lay in her sea power,
Her navy leaner and fitter by the hour.
John Hawkins' shipbuilding programme, slow but steady,
Was reaching fruition. The English were ready.
Spanish ships were still built to carry an army,
To disembark and fight on land (which was barmy),
Or in close combat. The sailors were simply crew,
Whereas those manning the English ships (this was new)
Were a force in their own right, one fighting unit,
Under expert naval command, eager and fit.
Spain's ships, slow and unwieldy in choppy waters,
Designed, as noted, for action at close quarters,
Were no match for the English vessels – low-lying,
Swift, mobile and light (which the Spanish found trying).

Spain's strength, however, should not be underrated –
Nor England's, by the same token, overstated.
Spain, remember, was a vastly wealthy nation,
Whereas England's frail financial situation
Had been further undermined by the Dutch campaign.
Despite her naval strength, there was little to gain
From launching an all-out offensive against Spain.
Warfare was expensive, and a risk. Then again,
As Spain re-armed, was England simply to sit back
And hope against the inevitable attack?
In what today would be called a terrorist raid,
Drake answered the question. Daring and unafraid,
Our around-the-world hero (Sir Francis, that is)
Sailed boldly into the Spanish port of Cadiz
And torched up to thirty vessels. All England cheered,
As the headlines screamed:
                    "Drake Singes King of Spain's Beard!"

Drake's triumph simply delayed the great Armada.
His message to the Spanish was, "must try harder".
Philip rose to the challenge and set a new date,
The attack now scheduled for 1588.
The King, however, already down on his luck,
Had barely rallied before new disaster struck.

His veteran Admiral of the Ocean Seas,
The Marqués de Santa Cruz, died and, if you please,
Philip appointed in the great Admiral's place
The Duque de Medina Sidonia – a disgrace.
Well, no, to be fair and to give the Duque his due,
He lacked experience, confessing (this is true)
That he'd rather tend his garden than go to war
And was regularly seasick. Need I say more?

Elizabeth's Admiral, on the other hand,
Was Howard of Effingham who, we understand,
Was a skilled commander of great experience.
Both Drake and Hawkins applauded Howard's good sense
And graciously served under him – no mean feat.

By July Philip's invasion plans were complete.
It's hard to say who had the superior fleet.
England fielded some two hundred ships, Spain fewer –
Though not by much. Several of Spain's were newer,
But they were galleons built in the taller style,
While the English design was better by a mile.
Effingham's force numbered some 16,000 men,
Compared to Spain's 27,000, but then,
Out of her entire force, a mere three in ten
Were nautical chaps. Infantry made up the rest –
All totally useless when it came to the test.

Spain's strategy, from the outset, was hit and miss.
Philip's plan of attack, in a nutshell, was this:
His fleet would sail directly to the Netherlands,
Where, even though most ports were in enemy hands,
It could ensure safe passage for Parma's large force
(A crack regiment) to England. Crazy, of course.
Such factors as Parma's good will, clement weather
And favouring tides all had to come together
For the plan to stand the faintest chance of success.
But Elizabeth's very survival, no less,
Depended on the outcome. The threat was still great.

Rhyming History

The seminal events of 1588 –
If you remember anything, make it this date –
Were a milestone in the fortunes of the nation.
They marked, moreover, a thorough vindication
Of the Queen's foreign policy: preparation,
Over decades, for war; naval reparation;
And a secure kingdom, of her own creation.

The Spanish Armada

On July the 19th the Spanish were sighted
Just off the Lizard. Effingham was delighted.
Three earlier attempts by his fleet to reach Spain
Had been frustrated by appalling wind and rain.
Holed up in harbour, he might have faced disaster,
But slipped out just in time (his ships being faster)
And harried the Spaniards as they made their way,
In tight formation, up the Channel. To this day,
No one is entirely sure how he managed it,
But Medina Sidonia, to give him credit,
Brought his great Armada to anchor off Calais
Without significant loss. There, I have to say,
His luck ran out. Parma's army hadn't arrived
And, if it had, would surely have never survived.

The Spanish plans lacked basic co-ordination.
Medina Sidonia's skilful navigation
Was nothing in the absence of Parma's support.
Spain didn't control one single deep-water port,
So the proposed link-up between Parma's forces
And the Armada was doomed. Those old war horses
Howard of Effingham, Seymour, Hawkins and Drake
Were quick to seize upon this strategic mistake.

On July the 28th, approaching midnight,
Six fire-ships sailed to set the Spanish fleet alight.
The latter (sitting ducks) broke rank and put to flight,
In panic. Medina Sidonia stayed to fight,

Off Gravelines, a bitter and costly battle.
His troops were outwitted and slaughtered like cattle.
Few ships were lost, though many were badly battered.
As for the rest (not that this very much mattered),
They were driven by gales blowing from the south-west
Into the North Sea and beyond. Sidonia's best
Proved inadequate, as England rose to the test.

The bad weather helped, but leadership was the key.
The Queen's great commanders proved masters of the sea.
All those years of privateering (nay, piracy)
Were paying dividends, and paying handsomely.
News of our victory only reached the nation
Some ten days later. Elizabeth's oration,
At Tilbury, in the shadow of invasion,
Was a thrilling and memorable occasion.
Although her body was a weak and feeble thing,
She had, she said, "the heart and stomach of a King" –
Moreover, she professed, "a King of England too".
And, though the persons present numbered but a few,

Her words were learned by heart by subjects yet unborn.
That "any Prince should dare invade" she thought "foul scorn".
The borders of her precious realm were sacrosanct,
And so it proved. England was saved. May God be thanked.

The Spanish fleet limped home. Half at the very most
Made it back to base. Wrecks littered the English coast
(The Scottish, too), blown to bits by the savage gales.
Some even foundered on the craggy coast of Wales.
"God blew and they were scattered," so the legend went,
As though the English victory was Heaven-sent.
Far from it, I should say. It was sheer bravery
That finally put paid to Spanish knavery.
Effingham's fleet lost fewer than a hundred men
And not a single ship. I should like to know when,
If ever, in the course of her long history,
England had won a more brilliant victory.

Elizabeth's last years

The twilight years of the Virgin Queen's splendid reign
Were a sorry anti-climax. The war with Spain
Was far from over. Philip was down but not out,
And Drake, in what proved to be a sad turnabout,
With Elizabeth's half-hearted blessing set sail   **1589**
With his own naval force (on an impressive scale)
To destroy what was still left of the Spanish fleet.
Delays and poor strategy guaranteed defeat.
Drake lost few ships, but he lost men – and he lost face.
The Queen was livid, and Sir Francis in disgrace.

The danger to England was never again as great
As when the Armada sailed in 1588.
Yet the Queen now found herself permanently at war –
A state of affairs she'd not experienced before.
The conflict with Spain rumbled on. On the high seas,
Privateers still won huge prizes but, by degrees,
Spain, as a nation, became a less urgent threat.
Not that open hostilities were over yet:
One battle, at Flores, in 1591,   **1591**
Saw the loss of the *Revenge*. The Spaniards won,
But Sir Richard Grenville's heroic resistance
Is the stuff of legend. With dogged persistence –
The *Revenge* stood alone – Grenville drew his last breath
In the service of his Queen, fighting to the death.

Trouble in France, meanwhile, reared its ugly head.
Huguenot fortunes there had reached a watershed.
The new King, Henry of Navarre (a Huguenot),
Was unpopular with Catholics at home, so –
In a move that smacked rather of desperation –
He sought help from abroad. Without hesitation,
Elizabeth offered him a generous loan
And a modest fighting force. It's never been shown
Why the Queen, who favoured peace, was quite so eager
To lend her support. Results were, at best, meagre.

After only a few months, the troops were withdrawn,
Weakened by illness, disenchanted and forlorn.
But in 1590, less than one year later,
Elizabeth again played the liberator,
This time in Brittany, where a small Spanish force
Was threatening the coast. In the event, of course,
The enemy menace was rapidly repelled,
But the French (a strategy in which they excelled)
Offered their English allies no support at all –
For a full five years! Henry even had the gall
(And gall it was) to request a second army
To fight more of his enemies in Normandy.

The Queen sent for Essex, an arrogant young fool,
To take command of this new force. Now, as a rule,
Elizabeth displayed remarkable judgement
In her choice of officers, and in government:
Walsingham, Cecil (father and son), Hawkins, Drake –
All living examples. Essex was a mistake.

The Earl of Essex

The young Earl's brief career is a sad history.
His appeal to the Queen was no great mystery.
Thirty-three years her junior, handsome and tall,
He held the elderly Elizabeth in thrall.
Some say that he stood for the son she never had,
And just as any spoilt child drives his mother mad,
So Essex 'dallied' with the Queen. He was skilful,
In his own charming way – demanding and wilful.
Daring on the battlefield, what can't be denied
Were his courage, bravado and personal pride:
Fine qualities in a fighter, rather less so,
Perhaps, in a commander. The Queen let him go.
Off he went to Normandy, twenty-six years old.   **1592**
Before the year was out, as many had foretold,
He'd failed, and returned to face Elizabeth's scorn.
She expressed the desire that he'd never been born.

The Queen's dissatisfaction, though, didn't last long.
Her dear boy soon bounced back. Essex could do no wrong.
A Privy Counsellor by 1593,
He soon enjoyed another opportunity
For 'fame in the cannon's mouth'. The long war with Spain,
After a dull patch, was livening up again.
Spain laid siege to Calais. A second invasion,   **1596**
So long feared, seemed imminent. On this occasion,
Elizabeth authorised a pre-emptive strike.
Essex may have been reckless, but (say what you like)
He was brave. The Queen's favourite was no coward.

Under four commanders – Essex himself, Howard,
Sir Walter Raleigh and Francis Vere – a great fleet
Sailed south as far as Cadiz. Victory was sweet.
The unfortunate town was sacked, plundered and burned,
Though to what purpose, who knows? When Essex returned,
With his popularity at an all-time high,
The Queen was lukewarm. Essex couldn't fathom why.
Philip had taken a hit and, for good measure,
Was bankrupt. But the fleet brought home little treasure.
Elizabeth was Henry Tudor's granddaughter –
Henry the Seventh – and one thing that he'd taught her,
By example, was that a successful nation
Gains by profit and wealth, not just reputation.

The ageing Philip, however, abhorred defeat.   **1597**
In the space of one short year he'd restored his fleet.
Essex (with the same co-commanders) again sailed,
Intent on death and destruction. This time they failed.
Incompetence, illness and other disorders,
Wilful disregard of Elizabeth's orders
(To attack Spanish ships), pretty awful weather,
And some degree of ill-luck, combined together
To turn the enterprise into a disaster.
Perhaps the fleet would have thrived under one master…
Be that as it may. The Queen's legendary rage –
Which was growing, if that were possible, with age –

Was given, on this occasion, its fullest vent.
The poor Earl already knew what her fury meant:
Lack of favour, political isolation,
Kicking his heels at court in idle frustration.

With Essex now, as it were, in hibernation,
Events moved on. To general consternation,
The French made peace with Spain in 1598.   **1598**
Was this the treaty that would settle England's fate?
Philip's unexpected death, though, in the same year
(At seventy-three) put paid to any real fear
Of a dangerous Franco-Spanish alliance.
Even when Henry of Navarre, the King of France,
Became a Catholic, nobody turned a hair.
Philip the Third of Spain, old Philip's son and heir,
Was a far more relaxed figure than his father,
Less prone to work himself up into a lather
Over foreign wars. Peace, though, in the Netherlands
Proved elusive. Still largely in Catholic hands
And under Spanish governance, it took some years –
Another half-decade of blood, toil, sweat and tears –
Before the native Dutch Protestant resistance
(In the north, anyway), with English assistance,
Drove out the forces of Spanish occupation.
Elizabeth's unbending determination
To offer succour to the persecuted Dutch
Was wise and politic. It mattered very much
That England continued to stand in defiance
Against any kind of Catholic alliance.

Old servants

In 1598 Lord Burghley (Cecil) died.
Forty years of service at her Majesty's side,
Unparalleled in the history of the age,
Was a long run on any political stage.
Francis Walsingham predeceased him by eight years,
Another sore loss to the Queen. Those privateers,

The Tudors

Sea-dogs Hawkins and Drake, both died in '95,
On an ill-fated voyage. Who was left alive?
Leicester was long gone. When he died in '88,
Elizabeth's grief was allegedly so great
That she shut herself up in her chamber, distraught,
For days. This revived all those old stories at court
That Robert was more than just the Queen's 'good friend'.

Poor Burghley had to break the door down in the end.
It is rumoured, when Elizabeth re-appeared
(Contrary to what her Privy Counsellors feared),
That she was quite composed –

              though her make-up was smeared.

Robert Cecil had long since succeeded Burghley,
His father. Robert was groomed for the job early,
Taking advantage of the vast experience
Of his *pater*. Most agreed that this made good sense.
Robert was able and adept, but well aware
(As were most others) that he lacked his father's flair.
Quite opposite in character was his rival:
Sir Walter Raleigh had to fight for survival.
An early favourite of the Queen, this young knight
Was handsome, a fine seaman, formidably bright,
A poet and essayist, and a man of wealth.
His tendency to think overmuch of himself
Led to a serious falling-out with the Queen,
When he married without her knowledge. As we've seen,

Rhyming History

Marriage was a sore point where she was concerned
And Raleigh knew, or at least he should have discerned,
That to wed one of her own ladies-in-waiting,
In secret, was tantamount to Bessie-baiting.
In what was hardly Sir Walter's finest hour,
He, and his sweet spouse, were marched off to the Tower –
Over-reaction by the Queen on a grand scale.
The happy couple's protests were to no avail.
In the end, Raleigh managed to buy their way out:
Money talking again, no shadow of a doubt.

I almost neglected to say that, long before,
Sir Walter (some time back in 1584)
Had founded the colony of Virginia,
But (can you imagine anything sillier?)
Had never gone so far as to set foot in it.

Back to the plot. After his release, bit by bit,
Raleigh regained his position in public life.
Royal favour was restored (though not to his wife)
And in '96, with Howard, Essex and Vere,
He sacked Cadiz, but shared, in the following year,
Their undistinguished drubbing at the hands of Spain.
The Queen never fully trusted Raleigh again.

Ireland

A sharp and nagging thorn in Elizabeth's side
Was Ireland. France and Scotland she took in her stride.
The Netherlands put her under permanent strain,
Personal and financial, not to mention Spain.
So her Irish policy took a poor fifth place,
And little wonder. The Irish were a disgrace:
Proud, rebellious and resistant to conquest.
Successive governors all tried their level best
To subdue the mutinous hordes, but failed the test,
Outwitted by the native chiefs who, unimpressed,

The Tudors

Scoffed at the alien notion of unity
And mocked the occupiers with impunity.

The Spanish eyed up Ireland as a likely base
From which to launch an invasion – a 'fertile' place,
Festering as it was with native discontent
Against the English. Elizabeth was intent,
Therefore, on conquering the Irish. No stranger
To conspiracy, she knew Spain, and sniffed danger.
Matters came to a head in 1598.
The Irish Earl of Tyrone, after quite a wait,
Inflicted in Ulster a resounding defeat
On the English, who seemed unable to compete.

I've read in a number of different sources
That the Queen starved her governors of resources.
This could well be true – I have no way of knowing;
But this much is certain: the danger was growing.
Ireland stood on the brink, a most perilous place.
Essex boldly announced, to Elizabeth's face,
That where others had stumbled, he could succeed.
The Queen, after some hesitation, agreed.

In the spring of 1599 off he went,   **1599**
With a fine new army and modern equipment.
His brief was to go to Ulster and stop the rot.
Essex had ample resources, but blew the lot.
He paraded through Munster (that's in the south-west)
In a display of strength that may well have impressed,
But did little to settle the Irish question.
Much given to conceit and autosuggestion,
Essex convinced himself that he, and he alone,
Was master of policy. He sought out Tyrone.
In contravention of strict orders from the Queen,
He opened negotiations. Tyrone was keen
(Or so he gave Essex to understand) to play ball,
But did he seriously want peace? No, not at all!

As the talks dragged on (which suited Tyrone just fine),
Essex's army fell into steady decline,
From boredom, discontent, desertion and disease.
Elizabeth, with a gnawing sense of unease,
Received this news from the Irish front. Her orders
Had been plain: for Essex to cross Ulster's borders
And engage the Irish in battle. This was war.
What else did Essex think that an army was for?

The fall of Essex

The Queen, in short, was livid. When Essex found out,
He deserted his post – a move which, beyond doubt,
Was a grand folly – and returned to plead his case,
In Elizabeth's royal presence, face to face.

Hot-foot from his tearful journey, picture the scene:
The frantic favourite and the furious Queen.
Excuses profited the former not a jot –
Scorn, derision and contempt were the Earl's sad lot.
Elizabeth made her displeasure very plain,
Refusing to see the young man ever again.   **1600**

Essex was arrested, charged, but cleared of treason.
He never fully recovered… lost his reason…
Became paranoid… all forces were against him…
His life was in danger… Then one night, on a whim,
In a moment of madness (and in the Queen's name!),
He wrested for himself one last moment of fame.
He raised a riot, progressing up Ludgate Hill
To the City. Elizabeth had had her fill.

To "overawe the Queen" was his avowed intent,
And nobody had any doubt what those words meant.
The foolish Earl had lost all sense of self-control:
Rebellion was high treason and heads would roll.

Essex was tried and convicted. He lost his head   **1601**
The following year. The wretch was better off dead,
In the opinion of those in government –
A focus of disaffection and discontent,
And a danger to the Elizabethan state.

Such was the unanimous view, at any rate,   **1602**
Of men like Cecil and Raleigh – even Bacon,
An old friend. Elizabeth was sorely shaken.
She had loved Essex, almost certainly too much,
But the boy had to go. The Queen kept her sure touch,
Even into old age. In June 1602
She addressed the French Ambassador thus: "I knew,"
She said, "that to indulge my own inclination
"Were against the best interests of the nation."

Economics and social policy

Yet the Queen was weary. Perhaps she'd had enough.
The last ten years had been particularly tough.
Plague and poor harvests (a lethal combination)
Led to soaring prices (we call it inflation).

Rhyming History

Low wages and high costs triggered social unrest:
The danger to the commonwealth was manifest.

The Statute of Elizabeth (1601)
Was a gem of legislation second to none.
Poverty and vagrancy had grown too widespread
For the Church to manage. So the Parish, instead,
Was charged with the onerous task of poor relief:
Charity for the sick, chastisement for the thief,
Alms for the aged and work for the indolent.
Parish relief gave rise to widespread discontent
In later days. The workhouse cast a long shadow
Over future generations. Those in the know,
However, will acknowledge, as accepted fact,
That the Welfare State stirred into life with this Act.

Elizabeth had her own worries about cash.
Her demands on the public purse were far from rash,
But all those foreign expeditions – extensive,
Urgent and unwelcome – were very expensive.
It's been estimated that twenty years of war
Cost the Queen a cool four million – maybe more.
She was forced to sell a quarter of all Crown lands
To help foot the bill. These passed into private hands.
For the rest, she was increasingly dependent
On the funds voted to her by Parliament.

This accounts for the steady growth in influence
Of the Commons, in particular. It made sense
For Elizabeth to seek supply from this source,
And members were far from oblivious, of course,
To their obligations in defence of the realm.
But who steered the Ship of State? Who was at the helm?
Queen or Parliament? There was no suggestion
Of the tail wagging the dog – not yet. The question,
Though, hung in the air – just one of those little things
That might well have served as warnings to future Kings.

The Tudors

The Queen had a strange fondness for monopolies:
Exclusive rights to deal in such commodities
As sugar, salt and starch – basic necessities.
She granted these commercial favours, if you please,
As gifts to favourites, or in return for fees –
One of Elizabeth's less worthy policies.

This right she pleaded by royal prerogative.
Parliament opposed her. Something had to give.
Some monopolies were merely irritating.
It was, for instance, hardly debilitating
That playing cards were subject to monopoly.
But others were administered improperly.
Feelings were starting to run high. The air was tense.
Monopolies meant high prices and it made sense,
Where their exploitation caused particular grief,
To press for their abolition. The Queen's belief,
Bred of precedent, was that she could ride it out.
But the Commons were determined. There was no doubt,
This time, that Elizabeth would have to back down,
And this she did. The prerogative of the Crown
Was a right subordinate to the common good.
This the Queen acknowledged, as a wise monarch should.
All 'bad' monopolies were forthwith abolished,
And those who exploited them roundly admonished.
Injured parties could take their grievances to law:
What else, men argued, was the legal system for?

The Queen ruled with the consent of Parliament.
That was the secret of good Tudor government.

With her royal authority put to the test,
Elizabeth addressed the Commons. Self-possessed,
And with humility, she spoke thus: "I have cause
"To wish nothing more" – here she left a little pause –
"Than to content the subject, which is a duty
"That I owe." In a speech of compelling beauty,

Her honesty shone through:
　　　　　　"Though God hath raised me high,
"Yet" (her simple faith here brought a tear to the eye)
"Yet this I count the glory of my crown that I
"Have reigned with your loves." She paused for effect again,
Then: "God hath made me his instrument to maintain
"His truth and glory." Wiser princes might there be,
But never one to love their subjects more than she.
Members then filed past to kiss the hand of the Queen:
A touching, historic and memorable scene.

This was the last great speech that Queen Elizabeth made.
In 1603, at peace with God, and unafraid,
She took leave of this world in her seventieth year,　　**1603**
And no loyal subject lived who failed to shed a tear.
On the 23rd of March the Queen, on her deathbed,
Had approved her successor. The next day she was dead.
She gave a sign (well, that's what Sir Robert Cecil said),
Willing that her cousin James Stuart should inherit.
James the First, as he became, was of no great merit.

The Tudors

Already King James the Sixth of Scotland, as of right,
He was vain and opinionated – though rather bright.

There were no Tudors left. James was the great-grandson
Of Henry the Eighth's sister, Margaret. No one,
I repeat no one, challenged his right to succeed.
James' weak and wilful son would make poor England bleed:
Charles, Mary Stuart's grandson – what more can I say?
But that's another story for another day.

Literature and music

I have been guilty of the commission
Of a mischief, one glaring omission.
The great golden age of Gloriana
Saw a flourishing of the arts: drama,
Poetry, music. William Shakespeare –
The dramatist supreme and sonneteer –
Led the field. Elizabeth was a fan.
The fine tradition of blank verse began,
And achieved perfection in Shakespeare's plays.

His fellow writers are worthy of praise:
Kit Marlowe, stabbed to death in mid-career
In a pub brawl, in his thirtieth year;
Thomas Kyd, his plays all blood and thunder,
Who died deep in debt, and little wonder.

Rhyming History

Marlowe and Kyd were promising playwrights,
Though both, in their way, over-fond of fights.

The most rare Church music you'll ever have heard
Was composed at this time by William Byrd.
Thomas Tallis was his great predecessor,
Orlando Gibbons his able successor.
Secular songs and madrigals flourished too:
Dowland, Wilbye and Morley (to name a few)
Were masters of the art of the four-part song:
Where the verse was easeful, the harmonies strong,
The lyrics romantic, they couldn't go wrong.

To name the painter of the age is not hard:
The miniaturist, Nicholas Hillyard.
The beauty of his portraiture is sublime.
If you don't know his work, seek it out! Find time!

In King Henry's time, the masters of verse
Were Wyatt and Surrey. You could do worse
Than to read their *Sonettes.* They led the way.
The sonnet in Queen Elizabeth's day,
Widely regarded as the perfect form,
Took pride of place as the poetic norm.
Spenser and Raleigh, Sidney and Shakespeare,
Were all great craftsmen. But the lyric sphere
Encompassed a broad range of poetry:
Pastoral eclogues, odes, allegory,
Song cycles, love poems, even satire.
It seemed the heart of England was on fire!
Spenser's *The Faerie Queene* celebrates
The life of 'Gloriana', vindicates
The Protestant religion, radiates
Wisdom and morality, and debates –
In allegory – such themes as Justice,
Chastity, Courtesy and Holiness:
Not unlike a 'state of the nation' play,
Though quite impossible to read today.

The Tudors

More accessible still is the sonnet.
Read this if you will, and think upon it:

   "How may the poet turn his sharpest wit
   "To forge the image of thy sovereign worth?
   "My fragile verses now are merely fit
   "For simple images of basest earth.
   "Once idle Time had written in thy face
   "Those lines that caused more eyes to weep than mine,
   "For those who ill perceived thy battered case,
   "Let them believe, from these, that grace of thine.
   "My humble words struggle alas in vain
   "To stem the grief belonging to thy death.
   "Our worldly loss is only Heaven's gain:
   "God save the soul of good Elizabeth.
   "Thy work is done. Now speed thee to thy rest
   "And take thy place, dear Queen, among the best."

So ended, then, the great Elizabethan age.
Enter King James of Scotland now to take the stage.

Bibliography

G. R. Elton, *England under the Tudors* (Routledge, 3rd ed. 1991)

Encyclopaedia Britannica (2010)

Antonia Fraser, *The Six Wives of Henry VIII* (Weidenfeld & Nicolson, 2007)

John Guy, *Tudor England* (Oxford University Press, 1990)

John Guy, *The Tudor Age* (in *The Oxford History of Britain*, ed. Kenneth O. Morgan – Oxford University Press, 2001)

Robert Lacey, *The Life and Times of Henry VIII* (Weidenfeld & Nicolson, with Book Club Associates, 1972)

Jasper Ridley, *The Life and Times of Mary Tudor* (Weidenfeld & Nicolson, with Book Club Associates, 1973)

David Starkey, *The Reign of Henry VIII: Personalities and Politics* (Vintage, 2002)

G. M. Trevelyan, *A Shortened History of England* (Penguin, 1959)

Neville Williams, *The Life and Times of Elizabeth I* (Weidenfeld & Nicolson, with Book Club Associates, 1972)

Neville Williams, *The Life and Times of Henry VII* (Weidenfeld & Nicolson, with Book Club Associates, 1973)

Penry Williams, *The Later Tudors: England, 1547-1603* (Oxford University Press, 1995)

A. N. Wilson, *The Elizabethans* (Hutchinson, 2011)